1962

This book may be kept

FOURTEEN

The Development of the
Social Security Act

EDWIN E. WITTE, 1935

The Development of the Social Security Act

A *memorandum on the history of the Committee on Economic Security and drafting and legislative history of the Social Security Act*

by Edwin E. Witte

Executive Director, Committee on Economic Security, 1934–1935

with a foreword by
Frances Perkins

THE UNIVERSITY OF WISCONSIN PRESS · MADISON, 1962

Published by
The University of Wisconsin Press
430 Sterling Court, Madison 6, Wisconsin

Copyright © 1962 by the
Regents of the University of Wisconsin

Printed in the United States of America by
George McKibbin & Son, New York City

Library of Congress Catalog Card Number 62–9264

Foreword

by Frances Perkins

Secretary of Labor, 1933–1945

The confidential memorandum on the history of the Committee on Economic Security and of the drafting and legislative history of the Social Security bill, which Edwin Witte left behind him, is an extraordinary document. In his systematic and painstaking way, Witte had kept a daily diary for his own guidance in conducting, as executive director, the study and research of the Committee on Economic Security appointed by President Roosevelt in 1934. He put the records of this diary into consecutive form so that it might be of use to others coming after him. Reading it at this time is for me a stimulating experience, taking me back over the twenty-five years which have elapsed to the time when what is now called the Social Security Act was in the process of being made.

It was a strange assignment that Edwin Witte had when he came to Washington in mid-summer of 1934 to act as director of the work of studying the possibilities and drafting an acceptable scheme for a social security act in the United States of America. The Committee on Economic Security had been appointed by the President and consisted of five Cabinet members close to him and clearly sympathetic to him and responsive to his desires. As Secretary of Labor, I was chairman of it, and I realize again in reading this memorandum how difficult was our task, not because there was opposition, but because there were so many varied ideas and plans about how such a program might be set up in this country. And then there was the Townsend plan which both drove us and confused the issue. Without the Townsend plan, it is possible that the old-age insurance system would not have received the attention which it did at the hands of Congress. However, to have accepted the Townsend plan would have been ridiculous and would have damaged the economy still further.

Witte came to do the hard, laborious, intensive work which these five Cabinet officers had no time or opportunity, or even the training, to do. We set up a technical committee, which proceeded to take on a lot of experts, and this was where Witte's headaches began. It was like driving a team of high-strung unbroken horses. The patience, the intelligence, the level-headedness, the amiability of Ed Witte was all that made possible a report and a set of recommendations based upon consideration of all of the facts as well as the actuarial and tax problems involved. The result was a plan which has proved itself practical and effective and yet amenable to amendments and administrative changes as they have been necessary over the last twenty-five years.

Witte's memorandum reflects some of the confusions which rose as the violent differences of opinion among the experts and advisors made themselves felt, but it does not entirely reveal his cool-headed understanding of human nature, his success as a mediator, and his constant drive and ability to get the facts translated into words of a bill which could go before Congress. Confused as it seemed, this combination of technical committee, advisory committee, and final authoritative Committee on Economic Security turned out to be an admirable technique. It eventually brought forth an administrative program in which all aspects had been canvassed by people with different lines of responsibility and different approaches.

The President was imaginative and his mind began to play over the whole subject. He constantly brought out new ideas that he thought would be good. He wanted the system kept very simple. Witte, who had drafted a great many laws for the State of Wisconsin, knew that nothing which has to meet the Constitutional test and arrange for the administration and distribution of money can be simple. Yet he gladly agreed to try to keep it simple. The President wanted everybody covered for every contingency in life—"cradle to the grave," he called it—under a social insurance system. Witte was sympathetic to this idea but also practical and doubtful of too ambitious and large a scheme. The President was all for stabilization of employment; it sounded so good. Witte at once saw that it was not necessarily a part of an insurance scheme and that in insurance the important thing is that it should be sound and practical. It was essential that the plan should be practical and should be based on knowledge of the needs of the country, the prejudices of the people, our legislative habits, and our political ways. As I look back on it, I think that we made many mistakes, just as Witte thought, but still I see no other way by which so much could have been done in so short a time. The committee itself, made up of Cabinet members, was the clue to the development of the program. It could be trusted to be of one mind because we were all servants of the President and committed to assisting him in this program.

Witte was admirable in his understanding of this situation, and his memorandum reflects not only his regret that he had not more time in which to write a really first-class scholarly report, but also his determination to get out something that would "do" in the five months that were before him, and then to see it through the Congress.

The distress of the country was so great at that time and the amount of unemployment so alarming that political considerations justified the speed with which the President asked the committees to work, and Witte responded magnificently to this. The problems which were before the committees and which Witte helped to resolve had to do with whether we should have a state-federal coöperative system or a federal system; whether we should have unemployment insurance premiums assessed wholly against employers or whether wage earners should also pay their share of the cost of unemployment insurance. Another problem about which there was great divergence of feeling was the question of merit rating. Should there be a flat contribution from all employers without regard to their particular industry, or should there be merit rating, allowing smaller premiums or contributions from firms with a low rate of unemployment and putting a larger premium or tax upon those with a higher rate of unemployment? The technicalities of the collection of taxes and the offset allowance to the States were a matter of dispute and disagreement in the advisory committees, but they were worked out extremely well by Edwin Witte and some of the technical people. The whole matter of health insurance was included in the original assignment, and a separate report was made on health insurance, recommending a health insurance bill. For the sake of passing the Social Security bill, we postponed the introduction of the bill on health insurance as the opposition was so great from the American Medical Association (principally) that it would have killed the whole Social Security Act if it had been pressed at that time. Old age insurance was bound to have a somewhat popular support in the Congress, and it was Witte's idea to put that first in the bill. It was an extremely complicated provision to write, however, as the necessity for providing benefits of a reasonable amount for people who were already close to the old age and retirement period was most difficult. But the Government of the United States is not an insurance company. And so it could be done.

Witte reports on all these matters in his confidential memorandum, but he can hardly convey the excitements and the strain of the period in which he took so great a part, for he was always the friendly person, never being upset by the opposition of some of his co-workers. When the report was finally made to the President and went before the congressional committees, Witte had a right to think that his work was over, but it was really just beginning. He had to explain it, word by word almost, to the House and Senate committees. This was a new type of legislation—nothing of the sort had ever come before the Congress of the United States before, and it took much explaining and much patience. Witte's day-by-day diary has enabled him to make it clear just how these things were done and just what the problems were and the way by which the congressional mind approached the problems. His long experience in the Legislative Reference Library in Wisconsin undoubtedly helped him to understand the legislative mind, but this memorandum makes it clear what the forces were. The book is fascinating for one who took part in this whole period. It is as though a cover had been lifted and one could look into a caldron in which the Government and people of the United States were moving around in response to a new idea, and one sees in the words of this memorandum exactly how these things are done and how they operate behind the scenes. Ed Witte has done future generations a great service in preparing this report, and as we greet the report I say "Hail and farewell" to him. We do it with gratitude, not only for the work that he did, but also for the record that he made.

Introduction

by Wilbur J. Cohen

Assistant Secretary of the Department of

Health, Education, and Welfare, and

by Robert J. Lampman

Professor of Economics

The University of Wisconsin

Edwin Witte wrote this book in 1936, while his experience as Executive Director of the Committee on Economic Security was still fresh in his mind. The unusual lapse of time between writing and publication requires explanation. The author transformed his diary of working notes into a manuscript at the request of the then Committee on Public Administration of the Social Science Research Council, which was sponsoring a committee of researchers in the study of governmental procedures. It is clear that Professor Witte wrote the "memorandum," as he called it, not with a plan for immediate publication, but rather for the use of the Social Security Administration and for the use of a limited number of scholars interested in case studies of how a major piece of legislation comes into being. To further these uses, several copies of the manuscript were placed in the library of the Social Security Administration and in a few other libraries.

In 1955 a plan was initiated, but not completed, to publish the memorandum in connection with the twentieth anniversary of the Social Security Act, and at that time Professor Witte, jointly with Wilbur J. Cohen (who had been Witte's assistant in the Committee on Economic Security work), reviewed the manuscript for possible publication, making some corrections and minor deletions. The question of publication was revived in 1960, shortly after Professor Witte's death, by a group of his associates, including Arthur J. Altmeyer, Wilbur J. Cohen, and Robert J. Lampman. This group, in collaboration with Mrs. Witte, made several decisions which have been carried out in the present publication. One decision was to ask Secretary Perkins to write a foreword. (On behalf of the group, Arthur J. Altmeyer made this request of her and she graciously consented to do so.) A second decision was to publish the memorandum with relatively little change from the 1936 version, leaving it in virtually the same form in which it was drawn while the author was close to "the scene of the battle." A third decision was to supply a few explanatory notes (these are indicated either by starred notes or by brackets) and to append several documents referred to by the author. One of these, the summary of recommendations on risks to economic security arising out of illness made by the Committee on Economic Security (a set of recommendations which President Roosevelt decided not to have published at the time), is here published for the first time.

It is our belief that the present volume will interest readers for several reasons. First, because it is about an exciting change in the structure of the American economy. The Social Security Act of 1935 marked the beginning of the federal government's participation in a broad range of social-insurance and public-welfare programs. This act has had implications for almost every American family and for many of our social institutions. The original set of programs has, of course, been modified and expanded many times since

1935, most notably by the addition of survivors' benefits in 1939, disability insurance benefits in 1956, and by extensions of coverage and size and duration of benefits in several programs, as well as by introduction of related programs.* By 1961 the total annual federal and state expenditures in the fields covered by the original act were over $20 billion. In 1961 over 15 million persons were beneficiaries of the old Age, Survivors, and Disability Insurance program and the average number of persons receiving Unemployment Compensation benefits was over 1.5 million. At the same time over 6 million persons were recipients of benefits under the several assistance programs, which include Old Age Assistance and Aid to Dependent Children.

The background of the 1935 law, therefore, merits the study of all persons interested in the history of the New Deal period and of those concerned with social security. Here is an "inside" account of how a conviction held by President Roosevelt and his advisers was translated into a concrete program. It reveals how and why many of the particular features of the law came into being and why some possible features were left out. It provides an instructive lesson in political processes, illustrating interplay of ideas and interests within an administration, relationships between a President and key persons in Congress, and the responsiveness of government to political pressures. It tells of compromises and "trades," of jealousy and betrayal, of sacrificial effort and selfless coöperation.

A second reason that this volume has interest for present-

*A readily available statement of legislative changes from 1935 through 1960 is offered in *Laws Relating to Social Security and Unemployment Compensation*, compiled by Gilman G. Udell (Washington: Govt. Printing Office, 1960). The *Social Security Bulletin* for August, 1960, was devoted to a review of this same period. Pertinent articles in this issue have been published as a 74-page booklet by the U.S. Department of Health, Education, and Welfare, Social Security Administration, under the title *The Social Security Act: Its First Twenty-Five Years*.

day readers is somewhat apart from its historical value. It provides, even at this distance, an intriguing example of how government can call up and use the resources and talents of "experts" to guide policy makers. Professor Witte recounts in detail the use of an outside staff, of a technical board of government experts, of an advisory council, and of a national conference. Most intriguing of all is Witte's account of his own role of expert. As Executive Director he played the key role in mediating between a Cabinet committee, which was in close touch with the President, and a range of specialists in a variety of specific problems.

In all of this work Witte was energized by a firm belief in the worth of a social security program, and he was strongly committed to the goal of preparing a bill that would be acceptable to the Congress and the Supreme Court as well as to the President.

This impassioned belief, which was shared by others in and associated with the Administration, explains in large measure the rate at which the bill-drafting proceeded. Witte arrived in Washington July 26, 1934, and congressional hearings started on the bill drafted by the Committee on Economic Security less than six months later, on January 21. The extent to which Witte departed from the role of a detached, "ivory tower," academic expert is, perhaps, most dramatically illustrated by his protagonistic role as witness for the bill in four days of testimony before the House Ways and Means Committee and three days before the Senate Finance Committee. Before the bill had passed the House and Senate and gone to the President for his signature on August 18, 1935, Witte had confronted and negotiated with most of the political forces in America.

A third reason that this volume has interest is that it tells a story in the first person; it is an autobiographical account of a remarkable adventure by a remarkable man. It tells how a man moved from Madison, Wisconsin, to the center of the national stage to play a key role and returned to his provincial home at the end of one year. Many of his friends and former students will find personal satisfaction in reading this account of "Mr. Witte goes to Washington." The choice of Witte for this key assignment was not, of course, a merely random one. His experience up to 1934, in which year he was forty-seven years of age, had admirably prepared him for the work he was called to Washington to do. Witte used to refer to himself as " a government man," one who had spent all his career working for a state government, a state university, or the federal government. His first job was as secretary to Congressman John M. Nelson in 1912–1914. This was followed by service as Statistician and later Secretary of the Wisconsin Industrial Commission, and as chief of the Wisconsin Legislative Reference Library (1922–1933). In the latter capacity Witte served as draftsman and researcher for countless pieces of Wisconsin legislation. Concurrently with his work in the Legislative Reference Library, he served as lecturer and professor at the Department of Economics of the University of Wisconsin. He was an active member of the American Association for Labor Legislation. He carried forward his own scholarly work in a number of fields. In 1932 his definitive study, *The Government in Labor Disputes,* was published. In 1933 he left the State Capitol for a full-time university career but was called back in the summer of 1934 to serve as Acting Director of Wisconsin's Unemployment Compensation law. In 1931 he made a study trip to Europe to observe social insurance and relief institutions. By 1934 Professor Witte was a veteran in the "expert" role and a recognized authority in the fields of labor legislation, social insurance, and public welfare.

Following his duty as Executive Director of the Committee on Economic Security, Professor Witte returned to the University of Wisconsin in the fall of 1935. He later served the federal government as a Regional Director and Public Member of the War Labor Board in World War II. His contributions as public servant, teacher, and scholar were recognized in many ways, principally by his election as the first President of the Industrial Relations Research Association in 1948 and as President of the American Economic Association in 1956.

Perhaps Professor Witte's greatest influence was on and through his students. He was primarily, and in the full sense of the word, a teacher. It is at the same time revealing to note how much the experience recounted in the present volume meant to him. In an address at Rosary College in 1956 he said, "I am a man who by this time has lived almost the Biblical threescore years and ten. It has been my lot, for good or ill, to have had a somewhat active role in quite a number of the developments of the period of my adult life. Of nothing I have done am I more reasonably satisfied than of the work I was privileged to do as Executive Director of the President's Committee on Economic Security, which sponsored the Social Security Act."

Witte continued his interest in the broad field of social security after 1935 until his death in 1960. He served frequently as adviser and consultant to federal and state agencies, he spoke to many groups on social security topics, and wrote voluminously on the subject. A list of articles written by him during the 1935–1937 period is found in Appendix IV. A companion volume to this one, scheduled for early publication by the University of Wisconsin Press, will present about thirty-five of his articles and papers, selected from the several hundred he wrote on social security topics over the period 1920–1960. This forthcoming volume will include a complete bibliography of his writings on social security.

This memorandum is published by permission of the Social Science Research Council, whose Committee on Public Administration sponsored its original production, and by permission of Mrs. Edwin E. Witte. We are pleased to acknowledge the careful work of Mrs. Jack Barbash, who prepared the index.

Contents

List
of
Illustrations

PART I

General
History
of Committee
and Act

BACKGROUND OF THE
ORGANIZATION OF THE COMMITTEE

The Committee on Economic Security was created June 29, 1934, by Executive Order 6757. [See Appendix I.] The organization of this committee had been under consideration for some time previously and was definitely foreshadowed in the special message of the President of June 8, 1934.[1] This, in turn, was a development from the introduction of the Wagner-Lewis bill[2] several months earlier.

This was a bill designed to induce the states to enact unemployment compensation laws. It provided for the levy of an excise tax of 5 per cent on the payrolls of employers of ten or more employees, against which an offset was to be allowed for payments made during the taxable year to unemployment insurance (or reserve) funds established pursuant to a state law which satisfied certain standards prescribed in this proposed national law. This bill was introduced in February, 1934, and was drafted by Thomas Eliot, the Assistant Solicitor of the Department of Labor. Hearings upon the bill were held before a subcommittee of the Ways and Means Committee of the House of Representatives in March, 1934. In these hearings, the bill was strongly endorsed by Miss Perkins, the Secretary of Labor, by William Green, President of the American Federation of Labor, and by such leading specialists in the social insurance field as Abraham Epstein, Paul Douglas, Dr. I. M. Rubinow, Dr. John B. Andrews, and Helen Hall; also by a number of well-known progressive employers, including Henry Dennison and Ernest Draper. Opposition to the bill was publicly expressed only by representatives of some business organizations and a few individual employers. At the conclusion of the hearings President Roosevelt addressed a public letter

1. 73rd Congress, Second Session, H.R. Document No. 397
2. H.R. 7659, 73rd Congress, Second Session.

to Chairman Doughton of the Ways and Means Committee, endorsing the Wagner-Lewis bill in principle and expressing the hope that it might be enacted into law before the close of the session.[3] Nevertheless, the subcommittee which conducted the hearings reported the Wagner-Lewis bill to the full committee without recommendations. No further action was taken on this bill and it died with the close of the session in June.

This result appears to have been due to diverse factors all operating in favor of delay. Much stronger opposition was manifested by employers than was disclosed in the hearings. The unemployment compensation measure was linked in public discussions with the Wagner labor disputes bill, and both measures were strongly protested by businessmen. Still more important in the ultimate fate of the Wagner-Lewis bill was the apparent weakening of the President on the desirability of immediate action. Various people seem to have gone to the President to point out alleged weaknesses in the Wagner-Lewis bill and to urge that the entire subject be given more careful study. Among the arguments presented to the President which seem to have impressed him greatly was the claim that the unemployment reserve funds would in time reach a figure of $20,000,000,000 or more and that such large reserves within state or private control would operate to increase the severity of depressions.[4]

3. Letter published in the *New York Times*, March 24, 1934.
4. Among the persons who brought this aspect of unemployment insurance to the President's attention at this time was Dr. Rexford Tugwell, Under Secretary of Agriculture. Control over the investment and liquidation of unemployment reserve funds, centralized in the federal government, was also strongly urged by a special committee of the Business Advisory and Planning Council of the Department of Commerce, of which John J. Raskob, former Chairman of the Democratic National Committee, and William A. Julian, Treasurer of the United States, were leading members; also by Prof. Alvin H.

The President seems also to have been impressed by arguments that the time was ripe for a more comprehensive social security measure than one dealing with unemployment insurance alone. There was pending in Congress at this time the Dill-Connery bill,[5] authorizing an appropriation of $10,000,000 per year to pay one-third of the costs of old age assistance extended by states to aged dependents. This bill passed the House of Representatives and came very near passage in the Senate. The Administration took no official position on this bill, but the President seems not to have been entirely satisfied with the measure. A number of supporters of the Wagner-Lewis and Dill-Connery bills who called on the President in May, 1934, were advised by him that he had about reached the conclusion that the best thing to do was to delay action on these bills, prepare a more comprehensive program in the interim before the next Congress convened, and then to push this program promptly to enactment in the early weeks of the first session of the next Congress.[6] The matter seems also to have come up at a Cabinet meeting in which the same conclusion was reached and all members of the Cabinet agreed, in advance, to support a program prepared by a committee to be appointed by the President and functioning in the months intervening before the next session of Congress.[7]

Hansen in a chapter on "The Investment of Unemployment Reserves and Business Stability" in *A Program for Unemployment Insurance and Relief in the United States*, published by the Employment Stabilization Institute of the University of Minnesota, 1934.

5. H.R. 8461 and S. 493, 74th Congress, 1st Session.

6. This information has been given me by Paul Kellogg, Editor of the *Survey*, who was one of the people who called on the President on this occasion.

7. My information about this Cabinet meeting is derived from references to this meeting which were made on various occasions by Secretary Perkins during sessions of the Committee on Economic Security. Miss Perkins very effectively used the pledges of support of the social security program made at this Cabinet meeting to

The Administration's decisions on this subject were announced in the special message of the President of June 8, 1934.[8] In this message the President developed the thesis that reconstruction and recovery must go hand in hand. He pledged a continuance of efforts at reconstruction through methods which were in no sense revolutionary, but represented merely "the way once more to known, but to some degree forgotten, ideals and values." He outlined as a foremost objective in all measures of reconstruction "the security of men, women and children," and stated that security concerns primarily three factors: a decent home to live in; the development of the natural resources of the country to afford maximum opportunities for employment; and "security against the hazards and vicissitudes of life." On the first of these aspects of security, he urged enactment by Congress of the housing legislation then pending; on the last two, he promised studies in the interim between the adjournment of Congress and the convening of the next Congress—a promise which he subsequently made good by the creation, respectively, of the Natural Resources Board and the Committee on Economic Security.

On the third aspect of "the security of men, women, and children," which the President called "the security of social insurance," he made the following specific statements:

Next winter we may well undertake the great task of furthering the security of the citizen and his family through social insurance.

This is not an untried experiment. Lessons of experience are available from States, from industries, and from many nations of the civilized world. The various types of social insurance are

---

hold all members of the Committee on Economic Security in line for action on this subject in the session of Congress opening in January, 1935.

8. See Note 1 *supra*.

6

interrelated; and I think it is difficult to attempt to solve them piecemeal. Hence, I am looking for a sound means which I can recommend to provide at once security against several of the great disturbing factors in life—especially those which relate to unemployment and old age. I believe there should be a maximum of cooperation between States and the Federal Government. I believe that the funds necessary to provide this insurance should be raised by contribution rather than by an increase in general taxation. Above all, I am convinced that social insurance should be national in scope, although the several States should meet at least a large portion of the cost of management, leaving to the Federal Government the responsibility of investing, maintaining and safeguarding the funds constituting the necessary insurance reserves.

I have commenced to make, with the greatest of care, the necessary actuarial and other studies necessary for the formulation of plans for the consideration of the Seventy-fourth Congress.

These statments were interpreted in the press and in Congress as a suggestion that no action be taken on the Wagner-Lewis or Dill-Connery bills during the current session and as a definite promise that the Administration would present a comprehensive program for social insurance at the opening of the next Congress.

ORGANIZATION OF THE
COMMITTEE ON ECONOMIC SECURITY

The Committee on Economic Security was not created until three weeks after the President's message of June 8, 1934. Intervening were the closing weeks of Congress, in which the President was unable to give further attention to this matter. The actual planning of the organization to be set up seems to have been done largely by Secretary Perkins, Dr. Arthur Altmeyer, the Second Assistant Secretary of

Labor, and Harry Hopkins, the Federal Emergency Relief Administrator.

Out of conferences among these proponents came Executive Order No. 6757 of June 29, 1934. [See Appendix I.] A tentative draft of this order was submitted in advance to the Attorney General by Mr. Hopkins, who in an opinion given the President on June 28, 1934, held that Title I of the National Industrial Recovery Act authorized the President to establish the Committee on Economic Security and the various subordinate agencies contemplated in this executive order.[9]

Four distinct agencies and a staff were provided for in this executive order. The responsible, central organization was the Committee on Economic Security, but the executive order also provided for the creation of two subordinate agencies, the Advisory Council on Economic Security and the Technical Board on Economic Security, and for an executive director and a staff to assist the Committee on Economic Security.

The Committee on Economic Security proposed in the tentative draft of the executive order which was taken to the President was to be constituted of the Secretary of Labor as Chairman, the Secretary of the Treasury, the Attorney General, the Secretary of Commerce, and the Federal Emergency Relief Administrator.[10] In the final order, pursuant to the President's express wish, the Secretary of Agriculture was substituted for the Secretary of Commerce. The duties of the committee were set forth in the executive order as follows: "The Committee shall study problems related to the economic security of individuals, and shall

9. This opinion of the Attorney General bears the Government Printing Office Serial Number 82695–34 and is entitled "Creation of Committee on Economic Security and the Advisory Council on Economic Security."

10. My information upon this point comes from Dr. Altmeyer.

8

report to the President not later than December 1, 1934, its recommendations concerning problems which in its judgment will promote greater economic security."

The Advisory Council on Economic Security was not named in the executive order, but provision was made for the subsequent appointment of its members in a clause which read: "The original members of which shall be appointed by the President and additional members of which may be appointed from time to time by the Committee." The duties of the advisory council were to "assist the Committee in the consideration of all matters coming within the scope of its investigations."

The third agency provided for was "a Technical Board on Economic Security consisting of qualified representatives selected from various departments and agencies of the Federal Government," to be appointed by the Committee on Economic Security.

Finally, there was a provision for an executive director, also to be appointed by the Committee on Economic Security, "who shall have immediate charge of studies and investigations to be carried out under the general direction of the Technical Board, and who shall, with the approval of the Technical Board, appoint such additional staff as may be necessary to carry out the provisions of this order."

In a letter written by the President to Mr. Hopkins shortly after the issuance of the executive order, he was asked to set aside $87,500 from F.E.R.A. funds for the Committee on Economic Security.[11] This amount was regarded by me,

11. The comptroller held that actual expenditures from this allotment could be made only on signature of the disbursing officer of the F.E.R.A. The Committee on Economic Security prepared its own payrolls, ordered its own supplies, and handled all its expense accounts, but all disbursements had to be formally approved by the Chief Clerk of the F.E.R.A. and were made by F.E.R.A. checks. Until the allotment of $87,500 was exhausted these disbursements were all charged to this special account; thereafter, they were all

9

while serving as executive director, as definitely limiting the total expenditures which might be made by the Committee on Economic Security and its subordinated agencies and all plans were developed accordingly. Had Congress promptly passed the Economic Security bill, as was expected, this amount would have proven sufficient. Because it delayed in doing so and it was necessary to continue a very considerable staff, it became necessary in February, 1935, to get additional funds. As it was uncertain how much longer the committee would have to function, it was decided not to ask for another definite allotment but, instead, to carry all expenditures of the committee as a part of the administrative expenses of the F.E.R.A., although the committee continued to function as a separate entity. The committee did not finally wind up its work until the Social Security Board came into existence in October, 1935, and its total expenditures were $145,000 (including the $87,500 originally allotted pursuant to the President's instructions).

On the same day on which the Committee on Economic Security was created, the President also created the National Resources Board,[12] three of whose members were also members of the Committee on Economic Security. This National Resources Board was given functions relating to the second of the aspects of social security discussed in the President's message of June 8, 1934, that of the development

included as a part of the administration expenses of the F.E.R.A. All employees of the Committee on Economic Security received appointments and took oath of office as employees of the F.E.R.A.

12. The National Resources Board continued, with a somewhat altered membership but with the same staff, the National Planning Committee created a year earlier. It had a much larger staff and larger allotments than the Committee on Economic Security, and made a much more extensive report. This report, however, was not followed by any proposed legislation. In June, 1935, the National Resources Board was replaced by the National Resources Committee, with the same membership.

of the natural resources of the country to provide maximum, continued opportunities for employment. Very evidently, the President originally conceived of the two committees as being closely related, and in the early stages of their functioning several conferences were held between the executive officers of the two committees with a view toward a close correlation in their activities. Some contacts were maintained between the two committees until they both made their reports to the President in January, but their actual relationships were never very close.

More directly affecting the work of the Committee on Economic Security was the action of the President in constituting what amounted to an informal committee on the immediate relief problem. This committee was never given any formal status, but throughout the late summer and fall the President met weekly with Mr. Hopkins and Secretary Morgenthau on the development of a new relief policy and program.[13] Originally, the working out of a new relief policy was considered within the sphere of the Committee on Economic Security and a considerable number of staff studies were undertaken with this in view. The Committee on Economic Security was never advised of any change in this respect but long before it made its report it

13. This informal committee had no staff, but a large number of people connected with the F.E.R.A. were engaged throughout this period in working up data on the work program advocated by Mr. Hopkins. This was at the time the major interest of Mr. Hopkins and of the F.E.R.A. members of the Technical Board on Economic Security. Earlier they apparently looked upon the Committee on Economic Security as a possible vehicle for getting this program before the President and Congress, but Mr. Hopkins was able to get the President to give more direct and immediate attention to this problem, resulting in the organization of the informal committee referred to above. Thereafter, the main interest of the F.E.R.A. people in relation to the Committee on Economic Security shifted to keeping it from "gumming up" the work program, rather than actually working out this program through the vehicle of the Committee on Economic Security.

was evident that it was not expected to deal with the immediate relief problem. In its report it dealt briefly with the subject and in effect endorsed the Administration's work program, but it had nothing to do with the details of that program.

BEGINNING OF ACTIVITIES

Executive Director

The executive director was not appointed by the Committee on Economic Security until nearly a month later, and the technical board was not formally created until a still later date. During this intervening month, one formal meeting of the Committee on Economic Security was held and there were frequent conferences between representatives of the Labor Department and the F.E.R.A. (the two departments considered to be most directly interested) over the selection of an executive director and members of the staff, the technical board, and the advisory council. All these activities centered in Dr. Altmeyer, acting for Secretary Perkins, who with the consent of the other members of the Committee on Economic Security assumed responsibility for getting the work of the committee actually under way.

Various persons were considered for executive director, and the author of this report was finally selected.[14] I was notified of my selection by long-distance telephone by Dr. Altmeyer on the afternoon of July 24, and I had had no previous indication of being considered for this position nor any contact with the organization of the Committee on Economic Security or the formulation of its program.

To accept the position it was necessary for me to procure

14. Other persons given serious consideration for the position were Dr. Edgar L. Sydenstricker, Director of Research of the Milbank Memorial Fund, and Dr. Bryce W. Stewart, Director of Research, Industrial Relations Counselors, Inc., both of New York City.

a leave of absence from the University of Wisconsin and also from the work I was doing in the summer of 1934 as Acting Director of the Unemployment Compensation Division of the Industrial Commission of Wisconsin (which at this time was beginning the administration of the Wisconsin Unemployment Compensation Act). I was advised that all the work of the Committee on Economic Security would have to be completed by the time Congress convened and that it would be necessary for me to get a leave of absence from my university work only for one semester. I made arrangements for such a leave and also for release from my position with the Industrial Commission within twenty-four hours after I received the telephone call from Dr. Altmeyer, and then proceeded at once to Washington, arriving on the morning of July 26. After talking over the entire matter at some length with Secretary Perkins and Dr. Altmeyer, I accepted the position offered me and became the first employee of the Committee on Economic Security.

In the President's message of June 8, there was a reference to actuarial studies already under way. This statement may have related to studies then being made for the Federal Coördinator of Transportation, in connection with the Railroad Retirement Act, but no data bearing directly on the contemplated social security legislation had actually been collected or any persons engaged for this work.

Quarters

After I accepted the position of Executive Director, I first gave attention to the matter of quarters, as Dr. Altmeyer advised me that there were no quarters to be had in the Labor Department. At his suggestion, I consulted Corrington T. Gill, Assistant Emergency Relief Administrator, who had been designated by Mr. Hopkins to act for him as a member of the Committee on Economic Security while he was in Europe. I found that Mr. Hopkins had given definite instructions before he left for Europe to furnish quarters to the staff of the committee in the F.E.R.A. (Walker-Johnson) Building. So the question of quarters was settled within a few hours after I arrived in Washington. Mr. Gill first made available to me his own conference room, thereafter the private offices of Mr. Hopkins and, on the eve of Mr. Hopkins' return, larger quarters on the third floor of the Walker-Johnson Building.[15] These offices were quite satisfactory, but at first some of the officials of the Department of

15. The Social Science Research Council was anxious to undertake an extensive program of research in the social insurance field. It conducted a conference on this subject at the Cosmos Club in Washington as early as November, 1933, and a second conference at the Hotel Washington in the spring of 1934. Louis H. Brownlow presided at this conference, with Dr. Altmeyer, Morris E. Leeds, John Dickinson, Prof. J. Douglas Brown, Davies Rowe (representing Mr. Nourse of the Brookings Institution), Bryce W. Stewart, Edith Abbott, Miss Anderson, Frank Persons, R. S. Meriam, John Gaus, Luther Gulick, Oscar Weigert, Prof. Leland, Mr. Lee, Mr. Taylor, and Meredith B. Givens the other persons in attendance. All arrangements for this conference were made by Meredith B. Givens, then connected with the Social Science Research Council, which has the minutes of this conference.

Prior to this conference, Bryce W. Stewart, at Givens' request, prepared a list of studies which might profitably be undertaken in this field. This list provoked a heated controversy between Miss Abbott and Stewart over the place of relief in a social security program. This controversy seems to have prevented definite approval of any projects and the group adjourned without ever being again convened. Givens and Stewart, however, thereafter revised the list of possible research subjects, in consultation with Dr. Altmeyer. By that time the organization of a governmental committee was under consideration and Dr. Altmeyer used this list in outlining to the President what the Committee on Economic Security ought to study. I did not know about this list until sometime after I got to Washington, but did make some little use of it in outlining the fields to be covered by various members of the staff. Subsequently, after the Committee on Economic Security had made its report, Mr. Givens revived the idea of extensive, privately financed research in the field of social insurance, and in the summer of 1935 the Social Science Research Council created its Committee on Social Security to undertake this research.

14

Labor felt that the quarters of the committee should be on "neutral ground," rather than in any of the departments represented on the committee and instructions were given me to try to procure other quarters. These were found in the Department of Commerce Building, but on the eve of moving I was instructed by the chairman of the committee (Miss Perkins) not to do so, as she felt this might be construed by Mr. Hopkins as an unfriendly act. The question of quarters never again caused any difficulties and the incident recited was almost the only one to come up which seemed likely to involve the committee in misunderstandings between the departments whose heads constituted the official Committee on Economic Security.[16]

Planning of Studies

Besides quarters, immediate attention had to be given to the studies to be undertaken and the selection of a staff and the technical board. In my first conference with Secretary Perkins, I was advised that the Committee on Economic Security would like to get a preliminary report by September 1, outlining the major aspects of the problem and a tentative program for action. I advised the secretary that this would probably prove an impossible date in view of the short time intervening, but I at once began the task of outlining in some detail the research work to be done, and of getting people for each project who could do the work in a short time.

Prior to the organization of the Committee on Economic Security, a lengthy outline for research in the social insurance field had been prepared in consultation with Dr. Altmeyer by Meredith B. Givens and Bryce M. Stewart, representing the Social Science Research Council. This proved of some

16. Early in the summer of 1935, when the total number of employees had shrunk to about fifteen, the offices of the committee were moved to the Washington Auditorium.

value, but I felt it necessary to consult also the people, both in and out of the Administration, who had some part in the development of the program to date or who were reported to me to have valuable ideas on the subject. I, consequently, devoted a large part of the month of August to such conferences. Among persons thus consulted, in addition to Secretary Perkins and Dr. Altmeyer, were: Dr. Lubin, Miss Lenroot, and Mr. Eliot of the Department of Labor; Professor Viner, Mr. Oliphant, and Mr. Eccles of the Treasury Department; Messrs. Tugwell, Tolley, Wilson, and Means of the Department of Agriculture and the A.A.A.; Messrs. Gill, Williams, and Myers of the F.E.R.A.; Donald Richberg of the National Emergency Council; Dr. Leiserson of the National Mediation Board; Professor Hansen of the State Department; Walton Hamilton of the N.R.A.; Miss Edith Abbott and Miss Grace Abbott of the University of Chicago; Professor Felix Frankfurter of Harvard University; Justice Brandeis; Professor Raymond T. Moley; Miss Beulah Amidon of the *Survey*; Abraham Epstein; Dr. John B. Andrews; A. A. Berle; Mayor La Guardia; Senator Wagner; Representative Lewis; Representative Ellenbogen; and a little later, Gerard J. Swope, President of the General Electric Company, John J. Raskob of the General Motors Company, and Walter C. Teagle of the Standard Oil Company.[17] Very contradictory advice was given me by the people consulted, but I still regard these conferences as having been distinctly worth while, as they served to rapidly acquaint me with the

17. Messers. Swope and Raskob were consulted at the express request of the President and Mr. Teagle because he was the chairman of the Unemployment Insurance Committee of the Business Advisory and Planning Council of the Department of Commerce. At this early stage both Dr. Altmeyer and I felt that it was inadvisable to consult the major leaders of organized labor or the executive heads of the principal employers' associations of the country, as it was expected that they would be named to the advisory council.

widely varying views entertained within the Administration circle and the difficulties to be overcome.[18]

The President was at the time on his Pacific cruise and did not return to Washington until near the end of August. En route he delivered a speech at Green Bay, Wisconsin, in which he renewed his pledge to present a comprehensive social insurance program to the incoming Congress.[19] After he returned to Washington, he soon gave us a conference to discuss the work of the Committee on Economic Security. This was attended by Secretary Perkins, Dr. Altmeyer, Mr. Eliot, and myself. The President gave us approximately an hour and received us most cordially. We reported to him that the committee had begun to function and expected to make a comprehensive study of all aspects of the problems of economic security. The President, on his part, gave us his ideas on the subject, but without insisting that the com-

18. There were, of course, many other occasions when there were differences of opinion between the representatives of the various departments represented on the committee. These were far more pronounced between subordinate officials in these departments than between their heads, who constituted the official Committee on Economic Security. At times, it seemed inevitable that I and the staff would be drawn into these controversies, but we were always able to maintain an independent status and to preserve friendly relations with all departments. These relations were particularly close with the F.E.R.A. and the Labor Department, both of which aided the committee in numerous ways and directly assumed responsibility for much work which the committee could have done itself only at considerable additional expense.

19. At the suggestion of Prof. Moley I prepared a draft of a rather long statement on the problems of economic security for the use of the President on this occasion. Instead of this long statement, the President made only a brief reference to the subject, amounting to little more than a repetition of the promise to present recommendations on social insurance to the next Congress at the opening of its session. This speech was followed by an immediate fall of approximately five points in stock market prices, which led some people high in the councils of the Administration (particularly Treasury officials) to desire to "soft pedal" economic security.

17

mittee should necessarily recommend what he deemed desirable. The views which he expressed on this occasion were very much the same as those which he had presented in his message of June 8, 1934. He felt committed to both unemployment insurance and provisions for old age security and also wanted the committee to explore thoroughly the possibilities of a unified (package) social insurance system affording protection against all major personal hazards which lead to poverty and dependency. He expressed decided preferences for state administration of unemployment insurance, but again stressed that the reserve funds must be handled by the federal government; also, that unemployment insurance should be set up to give encouragement to the regularization of employment. He also again stated that all forms of social insurance must be self-supporting, without subsidies from general tax sources, but the conversation developed that he understood that assistance from general tax revenues would have to be given to people already old and without means. He indicated, however, that he still held the view which he expressed when, as governor of New York, he signed the old age pension law of that state, to the effect that the only long-time solution of the problem of old age security lies in a compulsory old age insurance system.

When I assumed my duties as executive director, I assumed that the primary function of the Committee on Economic Security was not research, but the development of a legislative program to be presented to the next Congress. I assumed, also, that all questions of policy involved in the legislative program would be settled by the Committee on Economic Security and the President; further, that the statements made by the President in his message of June 8, 1934, were definite commitments, which the Committee on Economic Security and its staff were bound to respect as determinations of policies to be followed in developing its program. This conception of the committee's functions was strengthened by my early conferences with Secretary Perkins and the first conference with the President above noted. In my conferences in August on the program to be developed I tried to get a more detailed conception of what the President meant by the statements relative to a social insurance program in his message of June 8, 1934,[20] but aside from the few items noted in the account of the first conference directly with the President I learned nothing about his wishes and preferences beyond the general policies outlined in the message. Nevertheless, I continued to regard the task of the staff to be not so much to advise the technical board, the committee, and the President, but to carry out their policies. Beginning with the first meetings of the technical board and the committee, I, consequently, always put on the agenda the major questions of policy upon which it seemed to me essential that decisions should be reached at an early date. I also advised all the major staff members of my conception of the work to be done by the staff and the impression I had that we were bound to develop the program along the lines indicated in the message of June 8, 1934, and was assured by all of them that they shared my views and would develop their work accordingly. From the

20. The only persons I could discover who had discussed the economic security program with the President prior to the creation of the committee were Secretary Perkins, Mr. Tugwell, and Professor Moley. Plus these, I knew that he had consulted Mr. Hopkins and his Secretary Louis Howe, but neither was then in Washington. Later I learned that he had discussed the subject also with Gerard J. Swope, John J. Raskob, and Owen Young. At the President's suggestion, I then made a trip to New York to consult the first two of these industrialists, to get from them their ideas on what ought to be done, which they had previously presented to the President. In all conferences with the people who had discussed the subject with the President prior to the organization of the Committee on Economic Security, I got nothing more specific about what the President had in mind than he expressed in his message of June 8, 1934.

19

outset, however, some members of the technical board held a quite different view, conceiving the committee to be an agency to study the entire subject, with the understanding that nothing was to be considered settled.

This view was the one I was compelled to adopt because the technical board and the committee long put off making decisions on major questions of policy. In my first conference with Secretary Perkins, she expressed her concept of the committee's task by dividing it into two parts: (a) a long-time, comprehensive program embracing all phases of economic security, and (b) an immediate legislative program confined to items which it seemed wise to press for in the next Congress. This appeared to me a very sound concept, and I, accordingly, sought to direct the work of the committee toward these two objectives: a comprehensive program for economic security to be presented to the country but not for immediate action, and an immediate program to go to Congress to be elected in November at the opening of its first session in January. The committee's studies were made as inclusive as seemed possible of fulfillment within a few months, but major attention was given to the development of the immediate recommendations to be made to Congress.

Formal Statement of the Purpose and Scope of the Committee's Studies

At the first formal meeting of the technical board, held on August 10, 1934, I submitted a "Preliminary Outline of the Work of the Staff,"[21] which was discussed, somewhat modified, and agreed upon as the basis for beginning work. Open-

21. This and all other documents referred to in this report for which no published source is given in the notes are available only in typewritten form. All of these were included in the set of the *Reports of the Committee on Economic Security* which was given to each member of the committee and to the Social Security Board, subsequent to the completion of the work of the committee.

ing paragraphs of this outline indicate the general concept of the work of the staff—a statement which was adopted by the technical board and approved by the Committee on Economic Security at its meeting on August 13, 1934:

Economic security is a much broader concept than social insurance embracing all measures to promote recovery and to develop a more stable economic system, as well as assistance to the victims of insecurity and maladjustment. The interrelation of all these various approaches must be kept in mind throughout this study, and all proposals made by the committee must be weighed in the light of their effects upon economic recovery. Inasmuch as other agencies (the NRA, the AAA, the National Resources Board, etc.) have been established to outline and carry out policies and measures to promote recovery and to prevent a repetition of economic catastrophe, these subjects are assumed to lie outside of the primary field of the investigations of this committee, although the work of the committee should be coordinated with that of other planning agencies.

The field of study to which the committee should devote its major attention is that of the protection of the individual against dependency and distress. This includes all forms of social insurance (accident insurance, health insurance, invalidity insurance, unemployment insurance, retirement annuities, survivors' insurance, family endowment, and maternity benefits) and also problems of providing work (or opportunities for self employment) for the unemployed, and training them for jobs that are likely to become available. These several problems must be studied not only from the point of view of long time policy, but must be related to the present relief and unemployment situation.

In covering this field, studies need to be undertaken along the following major lines:

1. The facts of the present situation, with reference to the several hazards which confront the individual, including the costs of the methods of protection now available.

2. The possible different general approaches to the problem of providing security for the individual, with especial attention

21

to their economic effects, and including administrative possibilities.

3. The specific proposals for economic security, including all major forms of social insurance, work programs, etc.

4. The financial (investment) and fiscal provisions of the measures given serious consideration.

5. The constitutional and legal aspects of the program recommended for economic security.

The primary object of all studies to be made by the staff, in cooperation with the Technical Board, is to assist the Cabinet Committee in the development of a legislative program, rather than the collection of new information. The entire field outlined above should be covered in a general way, but particular attention should be given to proposals which the Cabinet Committee, at a later date, may wish to have developed.

ORGANIZATION AND FUNCTIONING
OF THE TECHNICAL BOARD

Membership

Prior to my arrival to Washington, Dr. Altmeyer had asked each of the members of the Committee on Economic Security to designate one or more persons in their departments to serve as members of the technical board and had given some thought to the selection of persons not connected with these departments, but in the government service, who would bring to the technical board specialized knowledge of some phase of the problems to be dealt with. Immediately after my arrival, all of these persons were formally notified of their selection as members of the technical board. Their appointment was announced in the same newspaper story (published about August 1) in which my selection as executive director was publicized. The following were the original members of the technical board, thus designated: Arthur J. Altmeyer, Otto Beyer, Thomas Eliot, Corrington T. Gill, Alexander Holtzoff, Murray W. Latimer, Isador Lubin, H.

B. Myers, Winfield W. Riefler, H. R. Tolley, Victor N. Valgren, Jacob Viner, and Aubrey Williams.

At the first formal meeting of the technical board, it was decided to recommend an enlargement of the board by the inclusion of the following six additional members, who were formally appointed at a meeting of the Committee on Economic Security on August 13, 1934: Walton Hamilton, A. H. Hansen, Wm. M. Leiserson, H. A. Millis, Herman J. Oliphant, and Stuart Rice. A little later, Edward W. Jensen, Executive Secretary of the Business Advisory Council of the Department of Commerce, was added to the board, and in November, Miss Josephine Roche, Assistant Secretary of the Treasury, who had previously been named as a member of the Advisory Council on Economic Security but, having entered the government service, more appropriately belonged on the technical board.

Relation to Executive Director and Staff

In the executive order creating the Committee on Economic Security, the relations of the technical board to the director and the staff were outlined in the brief statement that the studies and investigations were to be under the immediate direction of the executive director, but "under the general direction of the Technical Board." In this executive order, also, it was provided that the director should appoint such additional staff as may be necessary "with the approval of the Technical Board."

These relations were clarified through motions adopted at the meeting of the technical board on August 10, and at the meeting of the Committee on Economic Security on August 13. At the former meeting, a motion was adopted authorizing the executive director to employ members of the staff without further action of the technical board; at the latter meeting a motion (offered by the chairman) passed unanimously that the executive director be designated as

Secretary of the Committee on Economic Security and of the technical board, and that he should have "general direction of all of the work of the Committee on Economic Security." Thereafter I consulted members of the technical board constantly and never made any important move without, at least, conferring with Dr. Altmeyer, who was named chairman of the technical board at the meeting of the Committee on Economic Security on August 13, 1934. I also made a "Report on the Progress of the Work of the Committee on Economic Security" at the end of each month, of which a copy was furnished to each member of the technical board, as well as to each member of the Committee on Economic Security; but I did not formally submit appointments and similar matters to the technical board for advance approval.

Functioning of the Technical Board

An informal meeting, attended by most of the original members of the technical board, was held on August 4, and the first formal meeting on August 10. Thereafter, but one other meeting of the entire technical board was ever held. This occurred on September 26, at which time the board considered the preliminary report of the staff and determined that thereafter it should function through an executive committee and special committees on the major problems with which the Committee on Economic Security would have to deal. The following five committees of the technical board were then designated in a resolution adopted by the entire Board:

Executive Committee: W. W. Riefler, Chairman. Corrington T. Gill, Jacob Viner, Alexander Holtzoff, and H. R. Tolley.

Unemployment Insurance: A. H. Hansen, Chairman. William M. Leiserson, Jacob Viner, Thomas Eliot, and E. Jensen.

Old Age Security: Murray W. Latimer, Chairman. Otto Beyer, Stuart Rice, W. W. Riefler, and Victor N. Valgren.

Public Employment and Relief: Aubrey Williams, Chairman.

24

Corrington T. Gill, H. R. Tolley, Isador Lubin, and Herman J. Oliphant.

Medical Care: Walton Hamilton, Chairman. H. B. Myers, H. A. Millis, Alexander Holtzoff, and William M. Leiserson.

(When Dr. Viner retired from government service in December, his place on the above committees was taken by Miss Josephine Roche.)

It was also voted that the chairman of the technical board (Dr. Altmeyer) should serve *ex-officio* as member of all committees, and that the secretary (the executive director) should sit with all committees. Subsequently, another special committee was organized by the Executive Committee on Unemployment Reserve Funds, comprised of Messrs. Riefler, Viner, and Hansen.

After September 26, the technical board functioned through the above committees and through almost daily contacts by many of its members with the staff. The executive committee held numerous formal meetings to consider the recommendations to be presented to the Committee on Economic Security. All recommendations formally made by the director and staff were first presented to the executive committee, and also to the committee of the technical board concerned with the particular problem (unemployment insurance, old age security, etc.). Usually, these recommendations were considered in joint sessions of these committees of the technical board, which were also attended by all principal staff members. At these meetings there were lengthy and very free discussions by all persons present, but the members of the technical board were the only ones who voted on the recommendations to be made to the Committee on Economic Security, and only the recommendations as revised and approved by the technical board were submitted to the Committee on Economic Security, although the committee was advised of all dissents by members of the staff.

Minutes were kept of all formal meetings of the executive committee, and these show that such meetings occurred on September 27, 28, and 29; October 12, 16, 19, 25, and 30; November 2, 5, 8, 22, and 30; December 12, 1934, and March 4 and 5, 1935. Many of these were joint meetings with other committees of the technical board. Separate meetings were held on a considerable number of occasions by these other committees, which thereafter met jointly with the executive committee, to discuss and decide upon the recommendations within their respective fields to be transmitted to the Committee on Economic Security. In addition to the formal meetings, numerous informal meetings were held and some of the individual members of the technical board constantly functioned as consultants and advisers to the staff. All members of the executive committee of the technical board devoted a great deal of their time during the fall of 1934 to this work, with the exception of Mr. Tolley, who was generally represented at the meetings of the executive committee by Dr. Louis H. Bean. Messrs. Latimer and Hansen, also, were consulted almost daily by the members of the staff working in their particular fields, and Messrs. Williams, Leiserson, and Jensen only slightly less frequently.

The technical board made a formal preliminary report to the Committee on Economic Security at its meeting held on October 1, 1934, and another formal report on "Major Alternative Plans for the Administration of Unemployment Insurance"[22] which was presented and discussed at the meeting of the Committee on Economic Security on November 9. The executive committee and the interested special committees of the technical board also approved recommendations made by the director and the staff relating to old age security and medical care, and the executive com-

22. This report is published in full in the *Senate Hearings on the Economic Security Act*, pp. 329–31, and also in the *House Hearings*, pp. 874–76.

mittee the recommendations on security for children. Several members of the technical board (Dr. Altmeyer, Mr. Eliot, Dr. Viner, and Alexander Holtzoff) attended practically all meetings of the Committee on Economic Security, and other members of the technical board (Messrs. Riefler, Hansen, Lubin, Roche, Latimer, and Bean [representing Tolley]), attended the meetings concerned with the problems in which they were particularly interested. No final report was made to the Committee on Economic Security, but the executive committee of the technical board very actively participated in the final stages of the preparation of the Report of the Committee on Economic Security. After this report had been filed, all members of the technical board gave it their loyal support, and several (Hansen, Leiserson, Latimer) testified in support of the social security bill in the congressional hearings. No member of the technical board ever publicly (or, as far as I know, privately) expressed any dissent from any of the recommendations made by the committee.

SELECTION AND FUNCTIONING OF STAFF

Subjects of Study

From the outset, it was recognized that unemployment insurance and old age security were two major fields to which the staff would have to devote a great deal of attention. Hardly less important were deemed health insurance, public employment, and relief; and from the outset it was agreed that the committee would have to make careful actuarial studies of the costs of the various contemplated social insurance measures. Very early, also, it was decided to undertake studies of the social effects and management of large reserve funds, the financial aspects of the economic security program, and the problems of the security for children. At

27

a later date, employment opportunities and security for farmers and agricultural workers were recognized as other major subjects for study. Numerous other studies were undertaken by the staff, but never assumed the importance of those which have been enumerated.[23]

Selection of Staff

Dr. Altmeyer had given some thought to a staff prior to my becoming connected with the committee and turned over to me his suggestions, but he did not insist upon the appointment of anyone. Both he and Secretary Perkins, however, indicated that they felt it was desirable to avoid stirring up old controversies through the selection as staff members of persons definitely committed to one side or the other on the question of pooled unemployment insurance funds vs. individual employer reserves.

23. Among the more important of the miscellaneous studies were reports on invalidity and survivor's insurance by Miss Olga Halsey; on workmen's compensation by S. J. Kjaer of the U.S. Bureau of Labor Statistics; on standards for investments by S. R. Harris; and on life insurance in relation to social security by Professor Edward Berman of the University of Illinois. Many shorter reports were prepared by junior members of the staff (the largest number by Wilbur J. Cohen) summarizing briefly foreign experience with social insurance measures, statistical information bearing on economic security problems, and the major proposals for social security which commanded considerable support in this country (Townsend plan, the Deane plan, social credit, etc.).

Later, when the social security act was before Congress, the executive director and members of the staff prepared many memoranda relating to some feature of this bill or to some counterproposal, principally of an argumentative character, for the use of members of Congress and at their request.

A list of the more important reports and memoranda prepared by members of the staff was presented by the executive director to the Senate Finance Committee and appears on pp. 323–24 of its published *Hearings on the Economic Security Act*. All studies made for the committee were included in full in the sets of the *Reports of the Committee on Economic Security* supplied to all members of the committee and the Social Security Board. (See note 21 *supra*.)

To head the study on unemployment insurance, Dr. Bryce Stewart of the Industrial Relations Counselors, Inc., New York, was under consideration before I became executive director. I felt that he was well qualified for this task, and at once began negotiations to procure his services. It developed that he did not feel that he could leave his position and would consider only an arrangement under which his work for the committee could largely be done in New York, and under which he could use his own staff to assist him. Such an arrangement was objected to by some members of the technical board, but was finally made. Almost the entire research staff of the Industrial Relations Counselors, Inc., was placed on the payroll of the Committee on Economic Security, so that the arrangement in effect amounted to employing the Industrial Relations Counselors, Inc., to make this study.[24] At Dr. Stewart's suggestion, Merrill G. Murray, Director of the Minnesota Employment Service, was taken on as his principal assistant, and placed in the office of the committee in Washington. Dr. Stewart himself spent some time nearly every week in Washington, and in October and November almost as much time in Washington as in New York. Most of his staff did all of their work in New York.

The selection of someone to direct the studies in the field of old age security proved somewhat more difficult. It was agreed by everyone consulted that the best person in the field was Murray W. Latimer, who was unavailable because he was the chairman of the Railroad Retirement Board. Mr. Latimer, however, served the committee as chairman of the Committee on Old Age Security of the Technical Board, and throughout was in closest touch with the development

24. Dr. Stewart himself was never on the payroll of the Committee on Economic Security, pursuant to his express request. Instead, his staff was put on the payroll, with the understanding that both he and the staff would work simultaneously for the committee and the Industrial Relations Counselors, Inc.

of the program for old age security. On his recommendation, Professor J. Douglas Brown of the Industrial Relations Section of Princeton University was first offered the position. After some delay, Professor Brown found it necessary to decline, but agreed to serve the committee as a consultant. Throughout most of the life of the committee, particularly during the period of the staff studies, Professor Brown spent a part of each week in Washington, devoting his time to the problems of old age security.

When we lost out in getting Professor Brown on a full time basis, it was decided to put Mrs. Barbara N. Armstrong of the Law School of the University of California in charge of the old age studies. Mrs. Armstrong was one of the small number of people who were considered for staff positions prior to my selection as executive director. While I did not know her personally, I thought highly of her book* and deemed it advisable to have her come with the committee before it was decided exactly what she was to do. At first she was thought of in connection with unemployment insurance; but when Professor Brown turned us down, Mrs. Armstrong was placed in charge of the old age security study, with Mr. Latimer and Professor Brown as advisers.

To head the study of health insurance and medical care, Dr. Edgar L. Sydenstricker had virtually been selected prior to my designation as executive director. I gladly accepted this selection, as Dr. Sydenstricker was an old personal friend and the outstanding authority in this field. Dr. Sydenstricker felt that he could not give up his work for the Milbank Memorial Fund, and it was arranged, consequently, that he might maintain his headquarters for the study in New York. At his suggestion Dr. I. S. Falk, also of the Milbank Fund, was associated with him in this study. Arrangements were made under which we paid a part of the

*Insuring the Essentials: Minimum Wage, plus Social Insurance— A Living Wage Problem (N.Y.: Macmillan, 1932).—ED.

salary of both Dr. Sydenstricker and Dr. Falk; subsequently, because of objections of Mr. Milbank, this arrangement was altered so that the services of Dr. Sydenstricker and Dr. Falk were loaned to the committee, without their being on our payroll. Both, however, devoted most of their time to our work until July, 1935. During most of this period, they had no assistants, but in the last months a considerable number of people were employed to assist them in the studies, at the expense of the committee.

Studies in the field of public employment and relief were first suggested by the members of the technical board who were F.E.R.A. officials. At their suggestion, Mr. Emerson Ross of the F.E.R.A. was placed in charge of these studies. For a time Mr. Ross was assisted by a considerable staff, most of whom were paid by the F.E.R.A. Mr. Ross himself remained on the payroll of the F.E.R.A. and continued to perform some functions in that organization. No final report was ever made by him or his staff, due largely to the fact that, as hereafter recited, the immediate relief problem came to be regarded as outside of the committee's jurisdiction. Several valuable interim reports were made by Mr. Ross and his staff and all of his work was of practical value in connection with the development of the Administration work program.

The study of employment opportunities was undertaken at the instance of members of the technical board connected with the Department of Labor. The studies in this field were directed by Dr. Meredith B. Givens of the Social Science Research Council. Dr. Givens associated with himself a number of able people, most of whom were connected with eastern universities (Mrs. Eveline M. Burns of Columbia University; Miss Gladys Palmer of the University of Pennsylvania; Miss Jane P. Clark of Columbia University; and Dr. Ewan Clague of the Philadelphia Council of Social

Agencies). The reports of Dr. Givens and his staff were able research reports, but did not figure very much in the final report of the Committee on Economic Security.

In the field of security for children, arrangements were made with the United States Children's Bureau to undertake the necessary studies, with Miss Grace Abbott, former Chief of the Children's Bureau, as adviser. These studies were made under the immediate direction of Miss Katherine Lenroot, Acting Chief of the Children's Bureau, and Dr. Martha B. Eliot of the staff of the bureau.

A similar arrangement was attempted to be worked out with the Department of Agriculture in relation to the study of the problem of security for farmers and agricultural workers. Originally, people from the Department of Agriculture who were connected with the Committee on Economic Security gave some thought to crop insurance as a measure of social security for farmers, but they came to the conclusion that the A.A.A. served all purposes of crop insurance. Then their interest shifted to the effects of the social security program on farmers and the possibilities for benefiting agricultural workers through such a program. After some delay, Dr. Louis H. Bean was placed in charge of this study. Aside from two preliminary reports, however, nothing was done with this subject, except that the Committee on Economic Security indicated in its final report that this was one of the aspects of economic security requiring further study.

For the study of the problems connected with the large reserve funds which it was anticipated would develop in unemployment insurance and old age insurance, Mr. O. S. Powell, Chief Statistician of the Federal Reserve Bank of Minneapolis, was employed on a part-time basis. Mr. Powell spent half of each month throughout the autumn on this study at Washington. He was advised by the special committee of the technical board on unemployment reserve

32

funds and was assisted by Mr. Alan R. Sweezy of Harvard University, then connected with the Treasury Department.

For the study on the financial aspects of the various suggested measures for economic security, efforts were first made to get Professor Carl Shoup of Columbia University and later Professor Clarence Heer of the University of North Carolina. When neither of these men could be gotten, Professor George A. Shipman of the University of West Virginia was added to the staff of the committee. His major interests, however, proved to be in a different field, and Dr. Joseph P. Harris was then brought on from the University of Washington to undertake this study. Dr. Harris, in addition to making this study, also served as assistant director of the committee and after I terminated my connections with the committee in July, 1935, as acting director.

Administrative problems were considered a part of each of the major subjects of study. Rather late, some special studies were undertaken which related exclusively to administrative questions. All of the early principal staff members were economists, actuaries, or social workers, but later several political scientists were added—Miss Jane P. Clark, Dr. Joseph P. Harris, and George A. Shipman—primarily for administrative studies.

Constitutional and legal questions were at all times considered to be the responsibility of the counsel of the committee, Mr. Thomas Eliot.[25] Mr. Eliot also drafted the economic security bill and had direct charge of guiding this measure through Congress.

25. When disagreements developed over the recommendations to be made on unemployment insurance, various other persons also prepared memoranda on constitutional questions, particularly Mrs. Armstrong of the staff and Mr. Holtzoff of the technical board. In the determination of the recommendations of the Committee on Economic Security, questions of constitutionality played only a minor part, but they were stressed a great deal at all stages of congressional consideration.

No separate statistical division was at first envisaged, although some statistical studies were undertaken from the outset. Later, a statistical department of some ten people was organized to work with the unemployment insurance and old age security staffs and the actuaries of the committee. The principal work done by these statisticians was to estimate the volume of employment and unemployment and the probable financial results of varying provisions in unemployment compensation laws.[26]

An actuarial staff was contemplated from the outset but considerable difficulties were encountered in getting a satisfactory organization for the necessary actuarial work. The two major actuarial associations of the country early offered their assistance to the committee and Professor James W. Glover of the University of Michigan and Mr. M. A. Linton, President of the Provident Mutual Insurance Company and one of the outstanding actuaries of the country, were called in for consultation. At their suggestion, a plan was adopted of placing two actuaries on the staff of the committee and flanking them with a Committee of Actuarial Consultants, composed of the very top men in the profession, who would not consider full-time employment. This Committee of Actuarial Consultants consisted of Professor Glover as chairman, Professor L. Reitz of the University of Iowa, Professor A. L. Mowbray of the University of California, and Mr. Linton. As staff actuaries, the committee secured the services of W. R. Williamson, Assistant Actuary of the Travelers' Insurance Company, and Otto C. Richter, Actuary of the

26. These estimates were prepared under the direction of Robert R. Nathan, at the time connected with the Pennsylvania Emergency Relief Administration. The methods used and the conclusions reached were published under the title "Estimates of Unemployment in the United States, 1929–1935," in the *International Labour Review*, XXXIII (1), January, 1936. These estimates, I believe, overstated the real problem of unemployment and the Committee on Economic Security refused to accept them as in any sense official.

American Telephone and Telegraph Company. Messrs. Williamson and Richter spent approximately three months in Washington, and thereafter continued to be subject to call and were several times brought to Washington (during the congressional consideration of the social security bill) to give advice on the probable effects of proposed and contemplated amendments. The Committee of Actuarial Consultants held meetings in Washington on November 7 and 8 and on December 11, and passed on and approved the methods used in the statistical and actuarial calculations.

Originally it was thought desirable to create a publicity staff. This was never done. Only a few newspaper releases were given out by the committee and these were handled by Mr. Fitzgerald, the public relations officer of the Department of Labor. A small editorial staff, however, was employed, and the committee issued a number of booklets explaining various phases of the social security work. The failure to develop a real publicity service I now believe was a serious mistake, as it might have been possible to offset some very bad publicity given out by sources hostile to the committee's program.

Finally, the committee had a general office staff, of secretaries, clerks, and stenographers, and a few junior research workers, available to gather information needed to answer inquiries. Many such inquiries were received from members of Congress and others relating to social security. This phase of the work increased as more people became aware of its existence. Within a relatively short period the committee had a very voluminous correspondence, having to answer all letters relating to social security received by the President and the members of the committee, as well as a large volume of mail addressed to it directly. A large part of this mail related to the Townsend plan which at the height averaged about 1,500 letters a day. This was handled through form letters, but much of the correspondence required the individual attention of the director and the staff.

As I originally envisaged the work of the committee, a staff of not more than twenty-five people was contemplated, most of them specialists in a particular field of social security. Throughout the period of the preparation of the staff there was a strong tendency toward constant increase of personnel. Nearly all of the major staff members desired assistants not originally contemplated. They were allowed a free hand in selecting their assistants and the staff at the peak (November and December) was nearly four times as large as planned.

The policy of employing specialists wherever possible was adhered to throughout, although some people (particularly Dr. Walton H. Hamilton) counselled against such a policy. It seemed to me that, in the short time allowed for a final report, it was necessary to get the services of people who already were thoroughly familiar with the subject with which they were to deal. In retrospect, I am doubtful about this decision, although there might have been even greater difficulties with a less specialized staff. One difficulty met with in employing specialists was that the people we wanted all had other jobs, which they could not leave immediately. In consequence, it was not possible to really begin the work of the staff until about September 1, and, even then, several unsatisfactory part-time arrangements had to be made to get the people we wanted. Still more serious was the fact that nearly all of the specialists had their own ideas as to what should be done. No one was engaged who did not indicate a willingness to subordinate his own views to those of the committee and the President. Actually, however, this did not work out, and some of the principal members of the staff later on felt very hurt because their individual ideas were not adopted in toto. Another difficulty which developed was that the specialists employed set standards of perfection for their work which prevented completion of their reports in time so that they could be of maximum use to the committee. Only a few of the major staff reports were completed by the time that the committee had to reach its decisions.

Preliminary Report of Staff

In my first conference with Secretary Perkins, I was advised that the Committee on Economic Security desired to have, if possible, a preliminary report from the staff, with a tentative program for action, by September 1. This date proved entirely impossible, as most of the staff members did not begin work until shortly before September 1. September 15 was then set as the date for the preliminary report and all staff members were advised that they were expected to complete the preliminary survey of their fields and present their tentative suggestions before that date. To assist them in doing so, I prepared an outline of the principal subjects which it seemed to me should be covered in such a preliminary report. Then in the second week in September, a series of conferences was held which were attended by all of the principal staff members and by many members of the technical board, in an attempt to arrive at a unified program for presentation to the committee. These conferences disclosed wide differences of opinion regarding many of the recommendations to be made; moreover, it proved impossible to get any of the preliminary reports of staff members, except the report of the staff members working on problems of medical care, until the last days of September.

As meetings of the technical board had been set for the last week in September and of the Committee on Economic Security for October 1, to consider the preliminary report, I was compelled to somewhat alter the original plan for this report. In the end, I wrote all of the first part of this report (which I signed), and followed this by long appendices composed of the preliminary reports of the staff members, bearing their names.[27]

The first part of the preliminary report consisted of a rather detailed presentation of the "Need for Additional Measures for Economic Security" and my preliminary recommendations on a complete and immediate program for economic security. The factual statement was later separately mimeographed and widely distributed, under the title, "Preliminary Report of the Staff of the Committee on Economic Security," in response to requests for information on the problems with which the committee was concerned. The recommended program for action differed in some respects from the recommendations made by staff members in the appendices, as I was careful to point out in the main body of the report.

This preliminary report was first presented to the technical board. That board discussed this report in a meeting of its entire membership and then referred to its various subcommittees consideration of the sections dealing with the respective subjects, to formulate a program to be recommended by the technical board to the Committee on Economic Security. These subcommittees met with the staff members working in their fields and made their own comments and additional recommendations. These, in turn, were presented to the executive committee of the technical board, which, with the director, prepared the "Preliminary Report

27. This arrangement was rendered absolutely necessary by the fact that the entire preliminary report had to be mimeographed before the technical board and Committee on Economic Security meetings and the fact that several of the preliminary staff reports were not completed until the day of the first of these meetings. One major staff member, however, took great offense because my recommendations differed from those which she made and were given in the main part of the report, while her recommendation (like those of all other staff members) appeared in an appendix.

of the Technical Board." This was presented to the Committee on Economic Security at its meeting on October 1, together with the "Preliminary Report of the Staff."

At this meeting, the committee discussed at some length the preliminary report of the technical board, and then instructed the board and the staff to proceed with the studies as outlined and the further exploration and development of a legislative program along the general lines suggested in the "Preliminary Report of the Technical Board."

Final Staff Reports

In the executive order creating the committee it was definitely stipulated that the committee should make its report to the President not later than December 1. The chairman of the committee from the outset stated that this meant not only completion of the report but also of bills to carry out the committee's recommendations. Under the circumstances it seemed necessary that the staff members should complete their reports by November 1, and they were so advised immediately after the committee meeting on October 1.

Actually a large part of the month of October was spent in conferences with the executive committee and the Committee on Unemployment Insurance of the Technical Board, all concerned with the subject of unemployment insurance. None of the staff reports were near completion by November 1. Then followed the National Conference on Economic Security and the meetings of the advisory council. A few of the less important staff reports were completed by December 1. Most of the principal members of the staff had been engaged only until December 1, but it was necessary to continue their employment to complete their reports. Of the major reports only those relating to child welfare, employment opportunities, and the economic risks of illness were actually completed prior to December 24, when the committee orally outlined its recommendations to the President. All of the major reports were subsequently turned in, but the committee could not wait for them. A few of the minor studies were never completed.

The completed reports of the staff on the Committee on Economic Security took up more than a dozen large volumes of typewritten material. Many of these reports were exceptionally able productions, and all of them compare favorably with any work that had been done in this field in this country. Copies of the completed reports were delivered to the members of the Committee on Economic Security and a summary of the factual material contained in these reports is now to be published by the Social Security Board (which also has a complete set of the staff reports).* A list of all reports which had been completed by the time of the congressional hearings was presented by me to the congressional committees with the offer to supply copies of any of them to any member desiring the same. None of the members of the congressional committees, however, ever asked for a copy of any of the staff reports and I am not at all certain that any members of the Committee on Economic Security ever read any of these reports very thoroughly.

The staff influenced the report of the Committee on Economic Security through the preliminary reports which were discussed at meetings of the committee and through oral presentations made by some of the staff members at

*Social Security Board Publication No. 20, *Social Security in America: The Factual Background of the Social Security Act as Summarized from Staff Reports to the Committee on Economic Security* (Washington: Govt. Printing Office, 1937). This publication is 592 pages in length, carries a preface by Witte, and includes a compete list of the staff reports.—ED.

40

these meetings, but the completed, final research reports figured very little in the work of the committee.

THE NATIONAL CONFERENCE ON ECONOMIC SECURITY

Evolution of Idea

The executive order creating the Committee on Economic Security (as already recited) provided for an advisory council, to be composed of persons from outside of the government service, whose function it was to be to advise with the committee on the legislative program to be recommended. No clear conception of how the advisory council was to be constituted or what it was to do, however, had been formulated by the time I was selected as executive director.

Two very different kinds of an advisory council were under consideration: (1) a small group of representative citizens to actually sit with and advise the Committee on Economic Security; and (2) a large body, representative of all parts of the country, the primary function of whose members it was to be to conduct public hearings in their respective sections, with a view toward acquainting the public with the problems of social security. This question, of the kind of an advisory council to be created, was discussed at the first meeting of the Committee on Economic Security which I attended (on August 13, 1934). In this meeting, the consensus was that a large council should be organized, to function mainly as a publicity agency. The committee, however, felt so uncertain about what ought to be done in this respect that I was instructed to consult with a number of persons in New York and New England friendly to the Administration and the contemplated program of social security to get their views on this subject. I did this and received from everyone consulted the advice that a large council functioning as a body to conduct public hearings would almost certainly get out of control and might completely discredit the program.[28]

Thereafter, the thinking on the subject shifted again to a small advisory council that could genuinely function as an advisory body, plus a large conference to be held in Washington, primarily for publicity purposes. It was originally planned to hold this conference late in September, but the engrossment of everybody connected with the committee in getting out a preliminary report made this impossible. Doubt also developed as to whether any conference was desirable. At the meeting of the Committee on Economic Security on October 1 this matter, as well as the organization of the advisory council, was discussed at some length and it was decided to leave the question, whether a National Conference on Economic Security should be held, and, if so, when, to the President for decision.

This matter was taken up with the President by the chairman (Secretary Perkins) and he indicated that a national conference might be useful, but that he did not wish to address such a conference until the second week in November. He also indicated that he still considered an advisory council desirable and that he felt that this should be a small group consulting with the committee, but making no report of its own.

28. Professor Felix Frankfurter suggested that the best procedure was to forget all about the advisory council and to concentrate all efforts upon preparing a program which would actually be given to the President by December 1, after which he could call a large conference to which the governors of the several states would be asked to send representatives and in which he would acquaint the states with the recommendations he expected to make to Congress on this subject. This idea was not adopted, but I now believe that it would have been the best procedure.

The National Conference on Economic Security

Following this conference with the President, the date of November 14 was decided upon as the time for the meeting of the National Conference on Economic Security. Invitations were sent out for this conference over the signature of Secretary Perkins. The number of persons invited was limited to 150, because the President indicated that he preferred to address the conference in the Blue Room of the White House, whose capacity was restricted to this number. The invitations were spread over the entire country and included most of the people who were known to be interested in the problems of individual economic security and, particularly, those who had written on the subject. Due to the limited number of invitations which could be sent out, however, and the concentration of the people who had written on the subject in a few metropolitan and university centers, it was necessary to omit some of the people who should have been invited.

In accordance with the same general idea, it was deemed desirable to have all speeches at the conference made by specialists in this field who were not on the staff of the Committee on Economic Security or connected with the technical board. It was realized that this sort of a program would result in a considerable clash of ideas, but this was thought to be desirable as indicating to the public that the Administration had not yet decided upon the kind of social security program it was to present.

All meetings of the National Conference on Economic Security, other than the meeting at the White House, were held at the Hotel Mayflower. These meetings were open to the public and were attended by a great many people, who had not specifically been invited. Only the persons invited, however, were taken to the White House, where the President delivered a short address to them and conferred privately with the members of the advisory council, which convened on that occasion for the first time.

The program of the conference was a crowded one. The general chairman was President Frank P. Graham of the University of North Carolina, who had been selected to serve as the chairman of the Advisory Council on Economic Security. Following a general opening meeting, featured by an address of President Graham, the conference divided into round-table sessions on child welfare, unemployment insurance, provision of employment, old age security, and medical care, conducted both morning and afternoon. Late in the afternoon came the address and reception by the President, and then, in the evening, a concluding dinner meeting, at which addresses were delivered by Secretary of Commerce Roper, Mr. H. B. Butler, Director of the International Labor Office, Geneva, Switzerland, and Mr. Hopkins and Secretary Perkins of the Committee on Economic Security. Mr. Hopkins and Miss Perkins were the only persons connected with the committee who participated in the program of the National Conference.

On the day following, there were special meetings held by members of the staff concerned with unemployment insurance and old age security with persons invited to attend the National Conference who were deemed to be specialists in these fields. On this day also were held the first formal meetings of the Advisory Council on Economic Security and the Medical Advisory Board, all of whose members were especially invited to attend the National Conference.

Results

The attendance at the National Conference on Economic Security was exceptionally large, although all persons in attendance, other than the specialists, had to pay their own

44

expenses. Nearly every person invited attended, including someone from nearly every state. The papers and talks at the conference were on the whole excellent. There was a considerable clash of views at the round-table sessions on unemployment insurance and on medical care, but this had been anticipated. The President's address seemed to most of the delegates, at the time they heard it, to be a strong one and the addresses at the dinner meeting in the evening were exceptionally fine.

Nevertheless, the National Conference on Economic Security seems to me now to have been badly handled, and its net effects harmful, rather than beneficial. At the conference and subsequently by letter, all persons invited were urged to present in writing to the committee any views which they might have on any subject related to economic security. However, some of these members of the conference felt that they had been asked to come to Washington for no purpose except publicity and felt slighted because they deemed themselves specialists who were not really consulted.

At the opening session the statement was made by the presiding officer, speaking for the Cabinet Committee, that it was not expected that any resolutions would be adopted at this conference, in view of the short time that could be devoted to each subject. Nevertheless, a resolution was offered in the round-table conference on unemployment insurance endorsing the Wagner-Lewis bill of the preceding Congress. This motion was entertained by the presiding officer and it was necessary for a representative of the committee to explain again that it was not deemed advisable to adopt any resolutions. This incident was played up in some of the newspapers as a rejection of the resolution which had been offered, although it was never voted upon.

The most unfortunate incident, however, occurred in connection with the President's address. In the report of this speech, the *New York Times* and the Associated Press (but none of the other news agencies) featured the alleged "turndown" of old age pensions by the President. This interpretation was based upon the sentence in the President's speech, "I do not know whether this is the time for any federal legislation on old age security." This sentence followed two paragraphs in which the President sympathetically discussed the need for provision for old age security and stated that he still held the view which he expressed when he signed the New York old age pension law, that the entire problem could not be met through gratuitous pensions, but called for the institution of an old age insurance system. The particular sentence played up in the newspaper accounts occurred in a paragraph in which the President stated that the problem had been made more difficult through organizations promoting "fantastic schemes which have aroused hopes that cannot possibly be fulfilled," but concluding that it should be possible "in time" to work out a sound program for old age security.

To the people connected with the Committee on Economic Security this statement meant merely that the President had not yet decided precisely what sort of program he would present on old age security, but that he still intended to include this subject in his recommendations to Congress, no less than unemployment insurance. The newspaper accounts referred to, however, played this up as meaning that old age security was not to be included in the program.

Immediately upon the appearance of the newspaper stories, Secretary Perkins gave out a statement that there was no justification for this sort of an interpretation of the President's speech. This was followed by a completely unfounded story in the *New York Times* to the effect that I had written the President's speech and that this had been submitted to the President by Secretary Perkins, who was very indignant with me because of the blunder.[29] Secretary Perkins wanted to deny this, but I felt that it was wisest to ignore the story. Thereafter, letters were sent by the committee to all persons who attended the National Conference, to the effect that the President's speech had been misinterpreted, and that he expected to include, in the Administration's program to be presented to the next Congress, both old age security and unemployment insurance. The President himself, two days after the National Conference, made the same statement, in a communication to the National Conference of Mayors. Yet many newspapers and even some people who attended the National Conference on Economic Security continued to interpret the President's speech as indicating the Administration's intent to do nothing about old age security.[30]

THE ADVISORY COUNCIL
ON ECONOMIC SECURITY

Membership

As has been stated, the advisory council held its first meeting on November 15, the day following the National Conference

29. *New York Times*, November 20, 1934. The facts were that I prepared a first draft of the President's speech but the paragraph in question read quite differently in this draft from that used by the President. The changes made by the President were probably intended to be verbal only but afforded some basis for the claim that old age security was to be shelved, although this certainly was not a necessary interpretation.

30. This version is included in the accounts of the development of the Social Security Act given by Abraham Epstein in the third edition of *Insecurity, a Challenge to America* and by Paul Douglas in *Social Security in the United States*, both published in 1936, although both of the authors attended the National Conference and received the letter from the committee stating specifically that the Administration intended to make recommendations on old age security, as well as on unemployment insurance. Mr. Epstein acknowledged receipt of this letter and expressed satisfaction to learn that the newspaper interpretation of the President's speech was incorrect.

on Economic Security. The membership of the council had been announced by the President ten days earlier, and the actual selections made a little prior to this announcement.

The selection of the members of the advisory council was made by the President from a list submitted to him by Secretary Perkins, prepared by Dr. Altmeyer and myself after consultation with the members of the committee and numerous others. Some thought was given to this matter before the Committee on Economic Security was created and the subject was at that time discussed by Secretary Perkins with the President, who indicated some decided preferences. Thereafter, Dr. Altmeyer kept a file of the names of persons to be considered for membership on the advisory council, constantly adding to this list as new names were suggested and getting all available information about the persons under consideration.

When it was decided (about September 1) to keep the advisory council a small body, the task became one of selecting a few of the persons under consideration. Professor Moley strongly urged the committee to limit the advisory council to not more than seven members or nine at the outside. An attempt was made to carry out this suggestion, but this proved impossible. One reason was that it was considered desirable to have an equal number of employer, employee, and public representatives. There were so many employers and, particularly, so many representatives of the public, who, it was thought, should not be left off the committee, however, that the contemplated membership had to be doubled. When the matter of actually appointing the advisory council was taken up with the President (in the last days of October) it was suggested to him that he appoint five employers, five representatives of organized labor, and from eight to ten representatives of the general public. In each group, approximately double the number of names of the persons to be appointed was submitted to the Presi-

48

dent, and he selected the ones he preferred. Thereafter, Miss Perkins wrote all of the persons selected by the President advising them that the President would like to have them serve on the advisory council and asking their acceptance. The actual appointments were not made until after receipt of the acceptances and were announced as a group.

The selections made by the President at this time were the following:

Frank P. Graham, president, University of North Carolina, Chapel Hill, N.C., Chairman.

Paul Kellogg, editor, *Survey*, New York City.

Gerard Swope, president, General Electric Company, New York City.

Morris E. Leeds, president, Leeds & Northrup, Philadelphia, Pa.

Sam Lewisohn, vice president, Miami Copper Company, New York City.

Walter C. Teagle, president, Standard Oil Company, of New Jersey, New York City.

Marion B. Folsom, treasurer, Eastman Kodak Company, Rochester, New York.

William Green, president, American Federation of Labor, Washington, D.C.

George M. Harrison, president, Brotherhood of Railway and Steamship Clerks, Cincinnati, Ohio.

Paul Scharrenberg, secretary-treasurer, California State Federation of Labor, San Francisco, Calif.

Henry Ohl, Jr., president, Wisconsin State Federation of Labor, Milwaukee, Wis.

Belle Sherwin, former president, National League of Women Voters, Washington, D.C.

Grace Abbott, University of Chicago, and former chief, United States Children's Bureau.

Raymond Moley, editor, *Today*, and former Assistant Secretary of State.

George H. Nordlin, Chairman, grand trustees, Fraternal Order of Eagles, St. Paul, Minn.

George Berry, president, International Printing Pressmen and
   Assistants' Union, Tennessee.
John G. Winant, Governor of New Hampshire.
Mary Dewson, National Consumers League, New York City.
Louis J. Taber, master, National Grange, Cleveland, Ohio.
Josephine Roche, Rocky Mt. Fuel Co., Denver, Colo.

Regarding these selections, the following comments seem
apropos: The selection of the chairman was given especial
consideration. In June, the President had indicated that a
man like Gerard J. Swope, or Owen D. Young, should be
selected as chairman. Secretary Perkins, however, felt that
no industrialist or trade union official should serve as chairman. This matter was further discussed with the President
and he agreed with the Secretary. It was then deemed advisable to get a chairman from the South, because it was
thought that the South was the section of the country in
which the social security program would have the greatest
opposition. It was primarily for this reason that President
Graham was selected as chairman, but a further consideration was that he was a genuine progressive.

It was deemed desirable that at least one of the employer
members should come from some other section of the country than the East. The President, consequently, selected as
one of the employer members, William P. Wrigley, Jr., of
Chicago, but he was not at home when Secretary Perkins'
letter reached his office, and his secretary gave such a curt
reply that at the last minute Walter C. Teagle was substituted for Mr. Wrigley. All employer members were selected
without consultation with any business organization. All of
these members, except Mr. Teagle, were connected with
firms which had experimented with voluntary unemployment insurance plans. Mr. Teagle was selected because he
was the chairman of the Unemployment Insurance Committee of the Business Advisory and Planning Council of the
Department of Commerce.

50

The labor representatives, similarly, were selected without consultation with the American Federation of Labor. To my knowledge, no one connected with the committee talked with President Green about the work of the committee until shortly before the National Conference on Economic Security. At that time, I outlined to him the kind of program we tentatively had in mind, and stated that we would give labor an equal number of representatives on the advisory council with the employers. Mr. Green was asked whether he could serve personally, but was not asked for any other suggestions. Messrs. Harrison and Berry were selected from membership of the Executive Council of the American Federation of Labor as being most likely to render really valuable service. Mr. Scharrenberg and Mr. Ohl were selected as representatives of the state federations of labor, and with a view to fair territorial distribution of the council memberships.

Of the members of the council who were representatives of the public, Miss Abbott, Professor Moley, and Miss Dewson were quite close to the committee from the outset. Mr. Kellogg was the personal choice of Secretary Perkins, who felt that at least one social worker should be a member of the council. Miss Roche likewise was a personal choice of Secretary Perkins, and while an employer was regarded as a public representative. Governor Winant was selected because he was a Republican and an outstanding liberal. Mr. Taber was selected by the President from a considerable list of farm leaders to represent the farmers' organizations; Mrs. Sherwin to represent the women's organizations. Mr. Nordlin was selected because of the great interest which the Eagles had long manifested in old age pensions. Aeries of the Eagles throughout the country adopted resolutions urging the President to appoint an Eagle to the advisory council. The committee at first was not inclined to recommend this, but upon further consideration felt that some advantages might be secured through doing so. Mr. Nordlin was selected from a considerable number of other Eagles under consideration because he had long been identified with old age pension work of this organization, and was, moreover, a state legislator.[31]

After the membership of the advisory council was announced, complaints were received from various sources that it did not include representatives of groups that should have been represented. Mr. Kellogg urged that there should be several persons on the committee who were in direct daily contact with the people in distress. At his suggestion, Miss Helen Hall, director of the Henry Street Settlement, New York City, and Joel D. Hunter, general superintendent of the United Charities of Chicago, were subsequently added to the committee.

Another complaint which led to additions to the committee concerned the fact that the original committee of twenty did not include a member of the Catholic faith. This was entirely unintentional, and when the matter was brought to our attention, we were under the impression that several of the members who had been named were Catholics, but this did not prove to be true. Father Burke of the Catholic Charities of the Diocese of New York went directly to the President to bring this matter to his attention, and the President assured him he would be glad to appoint a prominent

31. This appointment (or rather the selection of an Eagle as a member of the advisory council) gave great offense to Abraham Epstein, who formerly had been employed by the Old Age Pension Commission of Eagles and had left them after a bitter personal quarrel. This, I believe, was one of the major causes of the very hostile attitude which Mr. Epstein later developed toward the committee.

On the other hand, this appointment was very pleasing to the Eagles. Many of the Aeries of the Eagles adopted resolutions in support of the economic security bill after its introduction and got in touch with their member of Congress when, in March, passage seemed doubtful.

Catholic to the advisory council. I then suggested the appointment of Monsignor John A. Ryan, director of the Department of Social Action of the National Catholic Welfare Conference, an eminently qualified man. This suggestion was at once adopted, and Miss Hall, Mr. Hunter, and Monsignor Ryan were officially designated as additional members of the advisory council, prior to the National Conference on Economic Security.

Subsequent to this action, Father Burke presented to the President three names as representing the choice of a group of the bishops of the Church. These names did not include Monsignor Ryan. Fortunately, Miss Josephine Roche was at this time appointed an Assistant Secretary of the Treasury, and having entered the government service could no longer serve as a member of the advisory council (as stated above, she was then named as a member of the technical board, and of the executive committee of that board). This made possible the appointment of Miss Elizabeth Morrissey, of the College of our Lady of Notre Dame, Baltimore, as a member of the advisory council, from the list of persons suggested by the Catholic bishops.

As finally constituted, the Advisory Council of Economic Security consisted of twenty-three members. This was a much larger body than had been intended—something of a cross between the large and small councils which had been under consideration. This large membership rendered impossible the plan originally conceived of having the council sit with the Committee on Economic Security in its deliberations. Instead, the council functioned essentially as did the other advisory committees, but with a broader jurisdiction, embracing the entire scope of the committee's activities.

All members of the council were able and prominent people, but the majority of them had no specialized knowledge of any aspect of social security. It was a lay body,

53

rather than a group of specialists. Geographically, it was representative of every part of the country but half of the members came from New York and two-thirds from the East.

All members attended at least one meeting of the council, but Messrs. Berry, Harrison, Moley,[32] Scharrenberg, Taber, and Winant only a few meetings, while all other members attended every meeting. In the latter group were all five employer members, while there were never more than three labor representatives in attendance and usually only Messrs. Green and Ohl.

Meetings

The first meetings of the advisory council were held on November 15 and 16. These meetings were opened by an address of Secretary Perkins, in which she stated that the committee desired the advice of the council on the legislative program to be recommended to Congress, but felt bound by the preference expressed by the President that unemployment insurance should be developed on a coöperative federal-state basis. She urged the council in its consideration of alternative policies to seek to arrive at a unanimous decision, if possible. In the event of a division, she suggested that no formal vote be taken, but that the committee be advised how the several members of the council felt regarding the matter at issue. She specifically stated that the committee would give as much weight to the views of the minority as those of the majority, and explained that the executive order did not provide for any report from the advisory coun-

32. Professor Moley, however, was in closest touch with the committee throughout its entire period of existence. This included complete knowledge of everything that the advisory council was doing. He occupied, however, a very peculiar position, being regarded by both the council and the committee as a personal representative of the President. Consequently, he deemed it advisable to refrain from active participation in the work of the advisory council.

cil, but contemplated that the members should serve as advisors, collectively and individually, to the Committee on Economic Security. Finally, she stressed the great need for prompt action, calling attention to the fact that the committee was required by the President to make its report by December 1. She also urged that all information regarding the proposals which the committee had under consideration be treated as strictly confidential.

Following this address, the advisory council elected Mr. Kellogg as vice-chairman and the executive director of the Committee on Economic Security as its secretary. It then proceeded to a discussion of an extended memorandum, "Suggestions for a Long-Time and an Immediate Program for Economic Security," which I had prepared to serve as a basis for the beginning of the discussions of the council. In this memorandum, I outlined tentatively a possible program to be recommended by the Committee on Economic Security, pointed out the major alternative possibilities, and concluded with a list of questions on which the advice of the council was desired by the committee.

The discussions of the council in its first two days of meetings did not get beyond unemployment insurance, the first subject dealt with in my memorandum. On this subject, considerable difference of opinion developed on the same issues which had become subjects of controversy among members of the staff (type of law, employee contributions, governmental contributions, individual employer accounts, etc.). Members of the staff (Messrs. Stewart, Murray, Williamson, and later Mrs. Armstrong) were called upon to present their views, but neither at these meetings nor later did the council confer with the technical board or any of its members, although such a procedure was suggested by Secretary Perkins in her opening address. No member of the Committee on Economic Security attended any meetings of the council (apart from the opening address by the chairman), but Mr.

Eliot, Dr. Harris, and I attended all meetings and Dr. Altmeyer the first session. My role was confined to an attempt to present, as impartially as I could, the alternatives on all major issues and (with Dr. Harris' assistance) to keep full minutes of all discussions. Mr. Eliot attended to give legal advice and was also called on to present the arguments for the Wagner-Lewis plan of federal-state coöperation in unemployment insurance, being the only person not a member of the council to do so, while Mr. Stewart and Mrs. Armstrong presented the case for the "subsidy plan."

At the conclusion of the first two days of meetings, it was decided to create a committee on unemployment insurance to further study this problem, and to make a report on it to the entire council at meetings scheduled to be held on November 30 and December 1. This committee consisted of the chairman (President Graham), or in his absence, the vice-chairman (Mr. Kellogg), Miss Abbott, Mr. Folsom, Mr. Leeds, Mr. Green, Mr. Scharrenberg, and Governor Winant, of whom the two last-named were unable to serve.

This committee held several meetings beginning November 26, in which it attempted to draft a report on unemployment insurance, with the assistance of Messrs. Stewart and Murray of the staff. After two days' sessions, it reached the conclusion that it could not complete its work in time for the scheduled general meeting of the advisory council. At its request, I then postponed the next meeting of the council until December 6. Thereafter, the subcommittee held further meetings, but did not make any formal report. Instead, at its request, there was presented at the next meeting of the council a great mass of material prepared by members of the staff, giving their individual views upon the federal legislation to be recommended, an extended memorandum by myself on the "Major Issues in Unemployment Compensation," and practically complete drafts of federal and state

56

bills for unemployment compensation on the "subsidy plan," prepared by Messrs. Stewart and Murray.

By this time, the Committee on Economic Security had become worried because the date set for its final report had already passed and the President had advised all members of the Cabinet that Christmas was the absolute deadline for the presentation to him of any matter which they desired to have included in the Administration's legislative program for the coming session of Congress. At its meeting on December 4, the Committee on Economic Security instructed me to advise the advisory council, at the opening of its meeting on the 6th, that it was imperative promptly to complete the work of the committee and, specifically, that it hoped that the advisory council might be able to present its recommendations on unemployment insurance at the next meeting of the committee scheduled for noon, December 7. I did so and the advisory council, at the opening of its meeting on the 6th, decided to proceed at once to a decision on major controversial issues and voted that its committee on unemployment insurance should attend the meeting of the committee on the 7th to report orally the recommendations of the council.

The advisory council then took up in turn each of the major issues in relation to unemployment insurance, as I had noted them on the agenda for this meeting. On all matters decisions were reached without any votes or serious disagreement, except on the questions of governmental contributions, the rates of employer contributions, and the general type of the federal legislation to be recommended. On the issue of contributions from general tax revenues, the general consensus was against such contributions while there were still such great demands upon the government for the relief of persons presently unemployed, but Mr. Kellogg was so strongly of the contrary opinion that he never accepted this decision but on every occasion possible continued to urge

57

governmental contributions. On the rate of the federal tax on employers, the council recommended a rate of 3 per cent, after it had rejected motions for rates of 5 per cent and 4 per cent—the latter by a tie vote. On the type of the federal law to be recommended, the council adopted a motion to recommend the "subsidy plan," by a vote of 9 to 7, with one member present and not voting (Professor Moley), and 5 absent.[33] This issue of the type of federal law to be recommended developed considerable heat, which led, on the next day, to the adoption of a qualifying motion to the effect that this vote was merely to be taken as indicating the individual preferences of the members of the council, all of whom recognized that each type of federal law had distinct advantages and were satisfied to have the committee decide the issue.

Before this last issue (on the type of the federal law to be recommended) was decided, the Committee on Economic Security held its scheduled meeting (at noon on December 7) for receipt of the recommendations of the ad-

33. The members voting for the subsidy plan were Chairman Graham, Miss Hall, the five employer members, President Green, and Mr. Kellogg; those voting for the Wagner-Lewis plan were Miss Abbott, Miss Dewson, Miss Morrissey, Mrs. Sherwin, and Messrs. Hunter, Nordlin, and Ohl. Professor Moley was present but declined to vote. Messrs. Berry, Harrison, Ryan, Scharrenberg, and Taber were absent. The council voted that the members not present might subsequently record their vote on this issue. No one did so, but Mr. Taber at the council meeting the next day stated publicly that had he been present he would have voted for the Wagner-Lewis plan. Father Ryan was present during most of the debate on this issue but had to leave before the vote was taken. Before doing so, he stated that he favored the subsidy plan, but only if no attempt were made to set standards to which the state laws must comply, other than that they must use all funds received from the federal government for unemployment compensation, while the other members favoring the subsidy plan desired detailed federal standards to insure uniformity in state laws. In the *New York Times* story of the next day Father Ryan was included among those voting for the subsidy plan, but the vote was correctly given as 9 to 7.

visory council on unemployment insurance. The subcommittee on unemployment insurance of the advisory council attended this meeting in a body, but could make only a partial report because the council had not decided all issues considered. The members, moreover, disagreed among themselves over governmental contributions. Only Secretary Perkins and Mr. Hopkins of the members of the committee were in attendance, all other members being represented by subordinates. Most of the meeting was taken up by the discussion of inconsequential details, and its net result was to create a feeling on the part of the members of the Committee on Economic Security that the advisory council was getting nowhere and that the committee could not afford to wait longer for its recommendations, while at least some members of the council were confirmed in their idea that the committee would not take its recommendations seriously in any event.

The next morning (December 7), the *New York Times* ran a front-page story by Louis Stark in which the vote of the advisory council in favor of the "subsidy plan" was reported as an upset for the Administration's plans to recommend the Wagner-Lewis bill. In this account the debates in the previous day's council meeting were reported at some length and a list given of the members who, on show of hands, voted for the subsidy plan, without giving the names of the members on the other side or noting that six members were absent or did not vote. Publication of this story, which bore all the earmarks of having originated with someone who had attended the executive sessions of the advisory council, was a violation of the express request of the committee that no publicity be given to any of its deliberations.[34]

34. Who was responsible for this breach of confidence, I do not know. At the time I suspected Dr. Stewart, but newspapers credited the leak to President Green, who was a close friend of Mr. Louis

At this time also the Committee on Economic Security was informed that Dr. Stewart had consulted with members of the advisory council in advance of its meetings and had presented to them individually the case for the subsidy plan; also, that the employer members of the council had caucused in advance with Dr. Stewart and had reached an agreement upon a program to be supported by all of them.[35]

These developments all but terminated the usefulness both of the advisory council and of Dr. Stewart as far as their influence upon the report of the Committee on Economic Security was concerned. Both the report of the council and that of Dr. Stewart[36] were not received until the committee

---

Stark. I have since been told that the story really came from the Business Advisory and Planning Council, of which Mr. Teagle and Mr. Leeds were members, and for whom Dr. Stewart and the Industrial Relations Counselors, Inc., were acting as advisers, as well as for the Committee on Economic Security.

35. This caucus was held at the Hotel Shoreham on the evening of December 6, following a dinner given by Mr. Teagle. I was invited by Mr. Teagle to have dinner with him that evening and found that all the employer members of the advisory council were present, plus Dr. Stewart, and that the purpose of the meeting was to talk over the position the employer members should take on the several controversial issues affecting unemployment insurance. I excused myself as soon as I decently could do so following the dinner, but Dr. Stewart remained.

36. Only one copy of the final report of Dr. Stewart was supplied by him to the Committee on Economic Security, and a summary of his report was published in the *New York Times* before this copy was received by the committee. In this *New York Times* story, the differences between the committee and the "experts" were featured, as a discovery just made by the reporter. Dr. Stewart in his report favored an exclusively federal system of unemployment insurance and, as a second choice, the subsidy plan. His ideas were later incorporated in the Logan bill, S. 214, 74th Congress, 1st Session. After introduction of this bill, Dr. Stewart took no further important part in relation to the development of the social security legislation. With Abraham Epstein and others, he signed the Joint Statement to the Senate Finance Committee of February, 1935 (*Senate Hearings*, pp. 1138–40), urging substitution of a subsidy plan for the unem-

had practically decided upon its course of action and it gave them very little consideration in the final stages of the preparation of its report.

The advisory council held further sessions on December 8 and 15. On the first of these days, it gave some consideration to old age security and on the second to relief and other forms of public assistance. Principally, however, it was concerned with its final report, which was prepared by a drafting committee consisting of Messrs. Kellogg and Green and Miss Abbott.[37] The draft prepared by this committee was gone over in detail at the meeting on December 15 and a considerable number of changes were made therein by the council as a result of its discussions. It was then adopted without a roll-call vote and without being before the members in final form. Not until some days later was it finally completed and formally filed.

Report of Advisory Council

The report of the advisory council was furnished to all members of the Committee on Economic Security immediately after it was finally adopted. Thereafter, four supplementary reports (or statements) were filed by members of the council. Two of these were signed by the five employer members and Professor Moley and urged, respectively, that the contribution rates required from employers

---

ployment insurance titles of the economic security bill, and also made a few speeches critical of the Administration program, but dropped pretty much out of sight.

37. The actual work of drafting this report was largely done by Mr. Kellogg. He did not complete the report until after midnight of the evening preceding the meeting of the council on December 15 and the mimeographing was not completed until a few hours before this meeting. Later he intimated in a letter to me that the draft had been tampered with, but he worked all alone with the stenographers in getting it out.

should be reduced and that the employees should by the federal act be required to contribute at half the rates levied upon the employers. Another statement came from Messrs. Kellogg, Graham, Green, and Harrison, and Miss Hall and urged that contribution rates be increased, to make possible more liberal benefits. In another separate statement, President Graham outlined his reasons for favoring the subsidy plan. Besides these, several members of the council called in person upon the chairman of the committee to express dissent from particular recommendations of the council.

The final reports of the advisory council were not made public until the congressional hearings, although the major recommendations were correctly anticipated in stories published in the *New York Times*. I then presented the report and the several supplemental statements to both congressional committees and they were published in full in the *Hearings*.[38] Chairman Graham and Vice-Chairman Kellogg supplemented these reports by oral arguments before the Senate committee, in which they called attention to differences between the reports of the advisory council and the Committee on Economic Security, as did also Messrs. Folsom and Green and Miss Hall. References were often made before the Ways and Means Committee and in the halls of Congress to differences between the advisory council and the committee. Few members of Congress, however, I believe, really understood these differences and those who did realized that the major issue at stake was the degree of federal control. As the feeling in Congress was that even the proposals of the Committee on Economic Security embodied too much federal control, it gave scant consideration to the recommendations of the advisory council for greatly extended federal control.

38. *Senate Hearings,* pp. 226–37, 324–37; *House Hearings,* pp. 871–93.

Estimate of Functioning

In retrospect, it is very clear that the Advisory Council on Economic Security did not work out very well—due, I believe, to mistakes which we made in organizing and dealing with the council. The body was too large and too little time was allowed for its deliberations. The members of the council took their appointment by the President very seriously, and several had very distinct objectives in mind. The short time allowed for the council's deliberations doubtless gave many members the impression that they had been brought into the picture merely to serve as a "front," while being asked to act as rubber stamps. Professor Moley, Justice Brandeis, and Professor Frankfurter, among others, early warned the committee that an advisory council comprised of people brought together hurriedly without any specific knowledge of the subject and with little opportunity for "education" would prove a boomerang, particularly if it was a large group. As the situation developed, this proved to be the case. The council violated all requests of the committee, which, in turn, paid little attention to its recommendations. The loyal support given by the individual members of the council and the prominence of the entire membership offset to some extent these unfortunate results; but it remains doubtful whether, on the whole, it would not have been better to have had no organization of this kind.

From this experience, I have reached the conclusion that an advisory council with general jurisdiction is likely to function satisfactorily only if sufficient time is allowed for its deliberations. As an alternative, an advisory council of a very small number of persons sitting with the committee in all of its deliberations might have worked very satisfactorily, but the advisory council actually created proved very disappointing, despite the excellent qualifications of its

63

members and their sincere support of the cause of social security.

REPORT OF THE COMMITTEE ON ECONOMIC SECURITY

Functioning of Committee

The Committee on Economic Security held formal meetings, subsequent to my selection as executive director, on August 13, October 1, November 9, 16, 27, December 4, 7, 18, 19, 26, 1934, and January 7, February 15, and March 15, 1935. In addition to these formal meetings, there were several informal meetings in December, while the report of the committee was under consideration. These included an evening session of more than six hours at the home of Secretary Perkins, in which a final agreement was reached regarding the policies to be recommended. This meeting was held on either December 22 or 23, and was the longest and probably the most important of all meetings of the Committee on Economic Security. It was, however, not a scheduled meeting, no minutes were kept, and only three of the members of the committee—Secretary Perkins, Mr. Hopkins, and Secretary Wallace—were present, plus Dr. Altmeyer, Miss Roche, and myself.

Throughout the life of the committee, I had frequent conferences with the chairman (Secretary Perkins) and less frequently with Mr. Hopkins. These were the two most active members of the committee. On at least two occasions, I also had conferences in their offices with Secretary Morgenthau and Secretary Wallace, participated in not only by them but by a considerable number of their subordinates. More frequent contacts with members of the committee were made through their principal representatives on the technical board (who were members of the executive committee of that board). As already stated, I prepared and delivered to each member of the committee (and to each member of the technical board) a monthly report on the progress of the work, and at each meeting of the committee during the early stages there was considerable discussion of further plans. All details in developing these plans, however, were left to the chairman of the technical board (Dr. Altmeyer) and the executive director (myself).

Secretary Perkins attended all meetings of the committee, and Mr. Hopkins all meetings held after his return from Europe. Secretaries Morgenthau and Wallace attended most of the meetings personally and were always represented by one of their subordinates, if not present in person. Attorney General Cummings never attended a meeting, being always represented by Mr. Alexander Holtzoff, Assistant to the Attorney General. At every meeting every member was present either personally or through a representative (Viner, and later Miss Roche, for Secretary Morgenthau; Tugwell for Secretary Wallace; Gill or Williams for Hopkins; Holtzoff for General Cummings). Often members attending in person also brought with them one or more of their subordinates.[39] Invariably also, the chairman of the technical board, the executive director, and the counsel of the committee attended, and often other members of the technical board, who were called in because of their familiarity with a particular subject under consideration.

The chairman of the technical board, the executive director, and the counsel of the committee were the only persons who were selected directly by the committee for the work they did in its service. I was named before I came to Washington; Dr. Altmeyer as chairman of the technical board, and Mr. Eliot as counsel, at the first meeting I attended. The members of the technical board were formally

39. In addition to those mentioned, Sweezy of the Treasury Department and Bean of the Department of Agriculture attended several meetings of the committee.

named by the committee, but actually the committee merely ratified selections made by Dr. Altmeyer and myself and, later, by the board acting as a body.

Formulation of Legislative Program

As has been recited, I placed on the agenda of each meeting of the committee the major questions of policy which it seemed to me the committee would have to decide to formulate its legislative program. At each meeting it devoted some time to a discussion of these problems, but it did not reach even tentative decisions on any of them until November. At its meeting on October 1, it discussed quite thoroughly the preliminary recommendations of the technical board, but arrived at no conclusions other than that further study was necessary and that great care should be exercised to cause no undue alarm about the program.[40]

At this meeting the committee voted to hold one or more evening sessions on each major subject to be dealt with, as soon as the technical board and the staff were ready for such a discussion. It was understood that unemployment insurance should be the first subject taken up, but, unfortunately, the technical board and the staff could not agree on the recommendations to be presented to the committee, despite

40. In the summer of 1934 the Administration was very much concerned about the downward trend in industrial production. The suggestions of a comprehensive social security program were considered, particularly by Treasury Department officials, to be alarming to business, and many people closely connected with the committee were at this stage anxious to allay these fears. The technical board in its preliminary report strongly suggested the advisability of timing the entire program so as to have the coming into effect of its various parts geared to industrial recovery. This was accepted by the committee as a good idea and accounts for the provisions in its proposals designed to have them come into effect only very slowly. The jitteriness over the condition of business and the desire not to retard recovery also were factors in postponing the National Economic Conference and of any further pronouncement of the Administration's intentions until the middle of November.

their numerous conferences held during this month. Not until November did the technical board finally make a report on this subject and then only outlined the major arguments for each type of unemployment compensation law and indicated how the board and the staff were divided on this question. This report was considered by the committee at its meeting on November 9, which was attended by the principal spokesmen for each of the two major differing points of view. The committee after extended discussion reached the conclusions regarding unemployment insurance which were announced to the public by the President in his address at the National Conference on Economic Security. Similarly, the committee considered the recommendations to be made to the President on old age security at its meeting on November 27, those relating to public health and child welfare at its meeting on December 4; and at these meetings decided all major issues of policy involved in these subjects. In doing so, it had before it recommendations prepared by the executive director and the staff, which had been previously submitted to the technical board and revised in accordance with its suggestions. Likewise, members of the board and the staff were in attendance to explain the recommendations and answer questions.

Under the executive order, the final report of the committee was to have been completed by December 1, but it was not until December 4 that the committee had reached even preliminary decisions on all of the major subjects upon which it was deemed advisable to make recommendations. By that time the committee was very anxious to complete its work and felt that unless its recommendations could be placed in the hands of the President very soon, it would be useless to bring them in later, as the President had already begun final work on his legislative program for the incoming Congress.

The committee consequently instructed me (at its meeting on December 4) to bring the work of the advisory council and of the staff to an immediate conclusion and to prepare a preliminary draft of the final report of the committee, embodying the decisions already reached. Thereafter, on December 7, it received the partial report of the advisory council on unemployment insurance noted above, and on December 18, the final report of the council and later the supplemental statements of various members.

Long before that time the committee was deep in the work on its final report. My first draft of this report was completed about December 15, and formed the basis for the deliberations of the committee at its meetings on December 18 and 19 and the long informal meeting at the home of Secretary Perkins on the evening of December 22 or 23. In this meeting all parts of the program were reviewed and many changes made in details, necessitating a complete rewriting of the final report.

Final Report

At the informal meeting at the home of Secretary Perkins, agreement was reached on all essentials of the recommendations to be made to the President. At that time it was also decided that these recommendations should be presented at once to the President, both because he had set Christmas as a deadline for everything that was to be included in his message to Congress and also because all members of the committee felt that any formal report which they might make must be one acceptable in all details to the President (since Cabinet officers cannot well publicly differ from the President). This oral presentation of the committee's recommendations to the President was made on December 24, by Secretary Perkins and Mr. Hopkins. After a conference of several hours, the President accepted all the committee's program and stated that he would present it to Congress, with his recommendation for passage, in a special message to be delivered within ten days after the opening of the session.[41]

Thereafter the final draft of the final report had to be written. I prepared another draft of this report which was considered by the committee in its meeting held on December 28. At this meeting some further changes in policy were made, principally in relation to details. At another meeting on January 7 there again were changes and it was further decided that a complete bill to carry out the recommendations should be prepared and submitted to the members of the committee before they were asked to sign the final report. This involved a further delay of nearly ten days. The signatures of the members were finally gotten individually, the last of them on January 15. On that day the signed report was filed with the President, together with a draft of the economic security bill.

This final stage of the completion of the committee's report (after the President had approved its recommendations) was for me one of the most trying in my entire work for the committee. While the members of the committee were in entire agreement on all of the recommendations which were orally presented to the President on December 24, several of the members were unwilling to sign the report without having every word in the report and bill gone over by subordinates in whom they had implicit confidence or whose work might be affected. This brought into the

41. The President was under the impression at this time that the committee had completed its report. The members in speaking to the President used my first draft, but took it away with them, as it was not in final form. Subsequently, when the President came to write his message, his staff was unable to locate the committee's report, which he believed had been filed with him. I was then called at 1:00 P.M. to bring another copy of the committee's report to the White House. Even at that stage, the report was not yet in final form and had not been signed, but I delivered a copy as it then stood.

picture a considerable number of persons who had not been closely connected with the committee theretofore and who had no background for its recommendations. Many of them made criticisms of both the language used in the report and the policies recommended. It was necessary for me to see them individually and collectively and to make numerous changes in language to meet their particular objections.

No difficulty was encountered in the Department of Labor. The Secretary of Labor had been the prime mover in the organization of the committee and throughout kept in touch with all of its work. The one objective of Secretary Perkins at this time was to get a unanimous report, in agreement with the program which the President had approved. That in the end such a unanimous report was secured was due far more to her personal work with the other members than to all other causes.

Securing the signature of the Attorney General likewise created no problem. The Attorney General had instructed his representative, Mr. Holtzoff, to always go along with the Secretary of Labor. While he offered minor suggestions for changes, there never was any doubt of the action of the Attorney General.

Mr. Hopkins, the Federal Emergency Relief Administrator, and his subordinates on the technical board were in close touch with the work of the committee at all stages. Mr. Hopkins had some personal reservations about some of the recommendations, but once the agreement was reached at the home of Secretary Perkins, he raised no further questions of policy. With Secretary Perkins, he "sold" the committee's program to the President and rendered a most valuable service in this respect. Thereafter, he washed his hands of all details, delegating this task to Mr. Aubrey Williams, Assistant Federal Emergency Relief Administrator and a member of the technical board. Mr. Williams felt that the committee's recommendations were too conservative and did

70

not like some of the language used in the report. I rewrote the sections in question to suit Mr. Williams and then they were objected to by Secretary Perkins. Still greater difficulties developed over the drafting of the sections of the bill relating to old age assistance and aid to dependent children. Three or four extended conferences[42] were necessary and several different drafts of the parts of the bill in question had to be prepared, none of which was entirely satisfactory to the F.E.R.A. people. When it came to signing the report of the Committee on Economic Security, however, no difficulty at all was experienced with Mr. Hopkins.

Secretary Wallace submitted the draft of the final report which I had prepared to Rexford Tugwell, Under Secretary of Agriculture, Jerome Frank, Counsel of the A.A.A., and Louis H. Bean, a member of the economic staff of the Department of Agriculture. Mr. Bean was the only one of these men who had been in close touch with the work of the committee until then and he raised few objections to the report and none whatsoever to the recommendations. Dr. Tugwell and Mr. Frank, however, raised numerous objections, both as to policies and language. They did not like the coöperative federal-state system of unemployment insurance, desiring a national system instead. Since Secretary Wallace himself had voted for the federal-state coöperative system, and this had been accepted by the President, they

42. The principal participants in these conferences were Messrs. Williams and Ross and Miss Josephine Brown of the F.E.R.A., Jerome Frank of the A.A.A. (who at the time also acted as legal adviser of the F.E.R.A.), and Mr. Eliot and I of the Committee on Economic Security. Mr. Williams and Miss Brown both were strongly of the opinion that a federal department of public welfare ought to have been recommended and did not believe that it was sound to segregate the aged and dependent children for different treatment from others on relief. Mr. Hopkins also always was concerned that his charges, the people on relief, should not be "sold down the river," but recognized that differential treatment for different groups on relief would be desirable.

recognized that it was not possible to reverse this decision, but they desired to have the report state in effect that the comittee was uncertain whether this was the correct policy. I spent four or five hours of the evening of December 31 at the home of Mr. Tugwell going over the report in detail with him and Messrs. Frank and Bean. I left this conference with the impression that all differences had been straightened out, but on January 2 discovered that there still was no agreement. Thereafter, there was a conference with Secretary Wallace in his offices participated in by the Secretary, Mr. Frank, Mr. Bean, and still others (Dr. Tugwell dropping out of the picture). The Secretary seemed satisfied, but Mr. Frank still raised objections to the language used in the report. Numerous changes had to be made to suit Mr. Frank and at his insistence the provision which occurs in sub-section (6) of Section 903* of the Social Security Act had to be inserted in the bill. At one time during these first weeks in January, it seemed probable that the Secretary of Agriculture might file a minority report, at least this was repeatedly suggested by Mr. Frank. When on January 15, however, Secretary Perkins called on the Secretary of Agriculture for his signature to the completed report, she secured it without any difficulty.

Equally great, or even more serious, difficulties were encountered with the Treasury Department. There were two groups among the Treasury Department officials, neither of whom cared very much for the social security program: one a group of conservatives, who were anxious to keep down expenditures and to avoid alarming business; the other a group

*This section of the act had to do with the certification by the Social Security Board of state unemployment compensation laws. Sub-section (6) specified that in the case of such a state law, "all the rights, privileges, or immunities conferred by such law or by acts done pursuant thereto shall exist subject to the power of the legislature to amend or repeal such law at any time."—ED.

of radicals who felt that the measures proposed by the committee had little value.

Objections to the recommendations of the committee were in the last stages of the development of the committee's report made especially by Mr. Haas, director of the research of the Treasury Department. Mr. Haas was of the opinion that the old age insurance provisions recommended by the committee were unsound and Secretary Morgenthau shared this view. Further, he was dissatisfied with the recommendations on unemployment insurance, as he believed that the employees should be required to contribute as well as the employers. Secretary Morgenthau stated that he would sign the report, but only with a qualifying statement to the effect that he did not agree with the financing of the old age insurance program and favored employee contributions in unemployment insurance. His was the last signature to the report of the committee and was secured only after a personal appeal by Secretary Perkins, but was finally attached without any dissent or qualifying clauses.

An important factor in securing a unanimous report, I believe, was the fact that the President had announced in his first message to Congress on January 4 that he would present a special message on social security within ten days. The committee had "gotten the President out on a limb" and simply had to reach an agreement without further delay.

The fact that the members of the committee were all members of the Cabinet (except Mr. Hopkins whose relations to the President were as close as those of members of the Cabinet) was the strongest point in the organization of the Committee on Economic Security. Its members were such busy officials that they could not devote as much time to the consideration of the policies to be recommended as might perhaps have been desirable. They were all, however, of one mind in recognizing that they had to agree upon a program in accordance with the promises of the President.

73

The relations of the members of the committee to each other and to the President were such that, despite the numerous crosscurrents and dissents within their own departments, they were able at all times to present a unified front. Whether a committee differently constituted would have done as well, I doubt very much.

All troubles regarding the report of the committee were not over even when it had been signed and delivered to the White House. On the afternoon of January 16, after the President had already notified Congress that he would, on the next day, submit a special message dealing with social security, and after press stories on the message and the committee's report had already been given out at the White House, the President discovered a feature in the old age insurance part of the program which he did not like. This was the aspect that a large deficit (to be met from general governmental revenues) would develop in the old age insurance system after 1965, as was stated clearly in the press releases which were prepared by Mr. Fitzgerald of the Department of Labor. The President thereupon sent for Secretary Perkins, who, in turn, asked me to come over after the President had indicated that he could not support such a program. When I arrived, the President was still under the impression that there must be a mistake somewhere in the tables which appeared in our report. When advised that the tables were correct, the President insisted that the program must be changed. He suggested that this table be left out of the report and that the committee, instead of definitely recommending the particular tax rates and benefit schedules incorporated in the original bill, merely present these as one plan for meeting the problem which Congress might or might not adopt.

Following this conference with the President, all members of the committee were communicated with and all agreed that the President's wishes in that matter must be carried out. The report was again withdrawn from the President and changes made which he had suggested. It was not filed in final form until the morning of January 17, although it bears the date of January 15, 1935.

CONGRESSIONAL CONSIDERATION

The President's Message

The President sent a special message to both houses of Congress recommending legislation on economic security on January 17, 1935. With this message he transmitted the report of the Committee on Economic Security. In this message he urged that the legislation recommended by the committee "should be brought forward with a minimum of delay" and called attention to the fact that forty-four state legislatures were either then in session or would meet very soon and that much of the program recommended could be carried out only through supplemental state legislation. In addition, he summarized briefly the recommendations contained in the committee's report, and expressed concern that the federal legislation on unemployment compensation "should not foreclose the states from establishing means for inducing industries to establish an even greater stabilization of employment."

The first draft of the President's message on this occasion was prepared by Dr. Altmeyer, but there was nothing in this draft relating to the stabilization of employment. The President's statements on this subject came as a complete surprise to members of the committee, and reflected his oft-expressed personal views that unemployment compensation should be set up in such a way as to promote industrial stability. To the committee and informed congressional leaders, this statement meant that the President was not entirely satisfied with the committee's recommendations in this respect.

75

The President's message and the recommendations of the committee were well received by the entire country. They were praised by congressional leaders of all parties and in editorials in leading newspapers, with only a few dissents. The program recommended was acclaimed as sound and conservative, and most of the criticisms were that it did not go far enough. Only considerably later was any conservative opposition manifested. Very early, however, stories appeared regarding the dissent of the "experts" and the advisory council,[43] and as time passed more and more criticisms were levied at the program. By March, practically all newspaper and magazine comments were critical, although always with a note that the objectives sought were sound. Most frequently the criticisms centered upon the alleged lack of thorough consideration and the division among the advocates of social security, and concluded by urging delay.

The Drafting of the Economic Security Bill

A complete draft of a bill to carry out the committee's recommendations was delivered to the President on January 15, with the signed copy of the report. The drafting of this bill was largely the work of Thomas Eliot, the counsel of the committee. Mr. Eliot did some work in drafting particular provisions during October and November, but could

43. The earliest of these was a long story by Louis Stark in the *New York Times*, January 20, 1936. The purport of this story was that the committee had slighted the advice of the experts and completely disregarded the report of the advisory council. It also made very uncomplimentary statements about Secretary Perkins and myself. Like other *New York Times* stories referred to in this memorandum, this story bore every evidence of having come from someone in close touch with everything the committee was doing. The *New York Times* correspondents who wrote these stories, however, never came to the top people in the committee for information, yet wrote inside stories about its activities, which, while incorrect in details, had every appearance of authenticity.

do very little until the committee had reached final decisions as to policies, in December. In drafting the bill, he consulted the legal divisions of the Treasury on the old age insurance and some other provisions; the Children's Bureau and the F.E.R.A. on the child welfare sections; and the United States Public Health Service on the public health grants. Copies of the bill were delivered in advance to all members of the Committee on Economic Security, and some changes were made at the suggestion of Messrs. Frank and Wilcox, of the legal divisions, respectively, of the Department of Agriculture and of the Treasury. A copy of the bill was also submitted in advance to Senator Wagner, who, as well as his secretary, Mr. Keyserling, offered some suggestions for changes. The congressional draftsmen, however, were not consulted in the drafting of this bill, except for some incidental inquiries from the Senate draftsmen.

In the hearings on the economic security bill, the draftsmanship of the bill was severely criticized by members of Congress and by certain witnesses who testified on the measure. The most pointed criticism related to the fact that the bill made appropriations for various purposes instead of merely authorizing appropriations, as is the usual congressional procedure. This departure from the usual procedure, however, was not due to poor draftsmanship, but to a last-minute change in policy. When the President had accepted the committee's recommendations on December 24, he also adopted a suggestion made by Mr. Hopkins that the social security bill be combined with his work program. Subsequently, Mr. Bell, the Acting Director of the Budget, objected to this procedure and the President was persuaded that it was desirable to present the work program separately. Thereafter, the social security bill was worked upon as a separate measure, but we were advised that every effort would be made to get it through Congress at once after the work progress bill had been disposed of. It was expected that a special procedure would be followed in the House which would eliminate the necessity of two separate measures: an authorization act and an appropriation measure. Mr. Eliot drafted the bill on this assumption, but in the end no special procedure was adopted, and the bill was left open to the criticism that it violated the rules of the House governing appropriations.[44]

Other criticisms of bad draftsmanship were directed against the provisions relating to old age insurance. These were admittedly very imperfect, but again, Mr. Eliot was hardly at fault. No one had ever before attempted to draft language for an old age insurance plan in this country. Mr. Eliot had very little time to do so and, moreover, had to satisfy Treasury officials who had no sympathy with the plan and little knowledge of what was required. As it finally went in, the section incorporated the rates and benefits provisions which the President had stated would have to be revised before he could sign the measure. It was expected, consequently, by everybody connected with the committee, that the provisions on this subject included in the original bill would be revised and a substitute therefor prepared by the committee itself for later presentation to the Congress.

There was much criticism also over the omnibus character of the bill. This was voiced particularly by opponents of the proposal. The decision to present the entire program in a single bill was made by the committee and the President. It was felt that such an omnibus bill offered the best chance for carrying the entire program. I believe that this judgment was entirely correct. As the situation developed, I doubt whether any part of the social security program other than the old age assistance title would have been enacted into

44. My information upon the facts set forth in this paragraph was obtained currently from Mr. Eliot, except that relating to the original intent to combine the social security and work bills, which was given me by Mr. Hopkins.

law but for the fact that the President throughout insisted that the entire program must be kept together. Had the measure been presented in separate bills, it is quite possible that the old age assistance title might have become law much earlier. I doubt whether anything else would have gone through at all.

The arrangement of the bill was also a happy one. Mr. Eliot—acting on his own initiative—placed the old age assistance title first, because he felt that this was the most popular title. This proved to be correct, and the placing of this title first had the effect of drawing away opposition from the other titles, which had much less popular support.

Introduction of the Bill

Which members of Congress should introduce the economic security bill was a matter that was given some consideration by the committee and was finally referred to the President. A number of members of Congress early advised the committee that they would like to introduce the bill. The only senator among these, to my knowledge, was Senator Wagner, who was one of the authors of the Wagner-Lewis bill of the preceding session. In the House, however, there were a large number of members who asked to have this honor, among them Representatives Lewis, Ellenbogen, Connery, and Keller. The President settled the matter after a conference (on January 15) in which Secretary Perkins participated, as well as Democratic leaders from both houses (among them Speaker Byrns, Chairman Doughton of the Ways and Means Committee, Representative Lewis, and Senators Harrison, Wagner, and Van Nuys). The President at this conference suggested that the bill be introduced by the same members who had offered the Wagner-Lewis bill in the preceding session. Thereafter, Speaker Byrns advised the President that this was not satisfactory to Chairman Doughton. Whether the President then agreed that Mr.

Doughton, as well as Representative Lewis, might have his name attached to the bill, I do not know, but it is a matter of record that both Messrs. Doughton and Lewis introduced the bill in the House of Representatives.[45]

Further friction developed in the House over the committee to which the economic security bill should be referred. In the Senate, this bill went to the Senate Finance Committee, without opposition from anyone. In the House, the Speaker referred it to the Ways and Means Committee, to which it logically belonged. Chairman Connery of the Labor Committee objected and moved that it be referred to his committee instead. This motion was defeated after a rather bitter discussion. Subsequently, the Labor Committee conducted hearings on the Lundeen bill, and on March 15, while the economic security bill was still before the Ways and Means Committee, reported this bill for passage, by a vote of seven to six, the deciding vote being cast by Chairman Connery. Nothing further was done with the Lundeen bill. While it was on the House calendar, it never came to a vote, and no serious attempt was made to get a rule for its consideration.[46]

Congressional Hearings

All of the congressional leaders were strongly impressed by the President's insistence that the economic security bill should be enacted very promptly. They, accordingly, decided

45. I have been informed that Congressman Doughton did not even have a copy of the bill and could not introduce the measure until he had procured a copy of the bill introduced by Senator Wagner in the Senate. Nevertheless, the Doughton bill was given a slightly earlier number in the House than the Lewis bill, and the hearings in the Ways and Means Committee were scheduled on the Doughton bill, not the Lewis bill.

46. Congressman Connery introduced a resolution for a special rule for the consideration of the Lundeen bill, but this never came to a vote. There also was a petition for the consideration of the bill under the discharge rule, but only a few members signed the petition.

that hearings should be run simultaneously in both houses, so that the Senate committee would complete its hearings by the time that the bill passed the House.

Originally, it was intended to begin hearings in both houses on January 22. When the leaders of the House Ways and Means Committee learned that the Senate Finance Committee was to begin its hearings on that day, they insisted that the hearings must be started one day earlier in the House. It had been planned that Secretary Perkins, chairman of the committee, was to make the opening statement in both houses. Secretary Perkins had to attend a Southern Labor Conference (scheduled long before) on January 21. The House committee nevertheless, decided to go ahead with the hearings, and I had to make the opening statement before this committee,[47] while Senator Wagner was the first witness in the Senate. He did not attempt systematically to explain the several provisions of the bill, and I followed him on the stand for this purpose.

I testified for two days before the House committee and was then excused to appear before the Senate committee and thereafter spent the major part of two more days before the House committee. In my testimony before this committee, I was allowed to explain each title of the bill in my own way, before being subjected to questions. In the four days I testified, I pretty thoroughly covered the entire bill, after which others connected with the committee elaborated upon the parts of the bill with which they were particularly conversant. In the Senate, the same procedure was not

47. On the afternoon preceding the opening of the House hearings, Mr. Eliot and I spent three hours or more, at their request, with Chairman Doughton and Congressmen Hill, Vinson, and Cooper of the Ways and Means Committee, to familiarize them with the bill. This advance conference was very helpful to me in my testimony and gave these leading Administration members of the committee a head start in their knowledge of the bill.

followed and I was never able to make much of an explanation of the bill, being subjected to constant interruptions. Although I was on the stand before the Senate committee for the major part of three days, I did not get far beyond the first two titles of the bill, and no systematic explanation of all provisions was ever presented to this committee by anyone.

Arrangement had been made to have the Assistant Secretary of Labor, Mr. McGrady, take charge of the presentation of the case for the economic security bill. He followed up my testimony with other "Government witnesses": Secretary Perkins, Mr. Hopkins, Secretary Morgenthau, Miss Abbott, Miss Lenroot, Miss Roche, and Messrs. Latimer, Brown, Hansen, Leiserson, Nordlin, Green, Folsom, Epstein,[48] Story,

48. I had known Epstein for more than ten years before I became connected with the Committee on Economic Security and was a member of the advisory council of his Association for Old Age Security (later Association for Social Security) from its organization. Soon after my appointment as executive director he came to Washington, called on me, and expressed satisfaction at my appointment, as he did also in conversation with Secretary Perkins. On this occasion he discussed, in a most friendly manner, the recommendations the committee ought to make and informed me that he was writing an article for the *American Mercury*, to give us a complete statement of what he would do if he were running the Committee on Economic Security. (This article was published in the *American Mercury* for October, 1934, and sent to me in galley proof in advance of publication. In this article, Mr. Epstein urged that the committee not attempt too much and, specifically, advised against trying to include health insurance in the program.) Mr. Epstein's expenses on this trip were paid by the committee at his request, although he came to Washington without being asked to do so.

Thereafter, at my suggestion, Mrs. Armstrong, heading our old age insurance staff, communicated with Mr. Epstein to ask him to participate in a conference on the development of the recommendations to be made on old age security. Mr. Epstein had only recently been seriously ill, and the conference had to be postponed until late in October and was then held at New York, for Mr. Epstein's convenience. At his request, the committee extended an invitation to Dr. I. M. Rubinow to attend this conference, which he did. For the

and (John B.) Andrews, all but the last three named of whom had official connections with the Committee on Economic Security. A large number of witnesses interested in child welfare and public health, not connected with the

committee, Mrs. Armstrong, Mr. Latimer, and Professor Brown attended.

Mr. Epstein was one of the first persons asked to participate as a speaker at the National Conference on Economic Security. He was uncertain whether he would be able to attend (because of his recent illness), but was kept on the program and actually attended. He made one of the addresses at the round-table meeting on old age security and also attended the conference of "experts" on this subject conducted by the old age security staff on the day following the National Conference.

Next, Mr. Epstein came to Washington at the committee's request after hearings on the economic security bill had begun. This trip was made at my personal request, as I deemed it advisable to consult Mr. Epstein on the revision of the old age insurance title of the bill, which was necessitated by the objections of the President. Although Mr. Epstein had by this time already very sharply criticized the Committee on Economic Security in his magazine *Social Security*, he still appeared generally friendly to the committee. He spent an entire day in conference with Mr. Latimer and myself and then asked that I arrange that he be permitted to testify before both congressional committees among the "Government witnesses," to avoid the necessity of again having to come to Washington. He frankly expressed opposition to the tax offset plan for unemployment insurance (of which I was aware), but also stated that he wanted to go along with the committee as far as he could possibly do so. When I took up the matter of having him testify as a "Government witness" with Mr. McGrady, he expressed doubt regarding the wisdom of acceding to his request but finally did so, because I felt that it would tend to make Mr. Epstein more friendly.

On the stand, Mr. Epstein said some complimentary things about the President and the inclusiveness of the provisions of the bill, approved of the old age insurance sections, and then launched into a violent attack upon the bill, centering upon the unemployment insurance titles, the omnibus character of the bill, and the lack of adequate consideration.

Untoward circumstances which occurred during Mr. Epstein's testimony before the Ways and Means Committee may have contributed to the very extreme position which he took thereafter in opposition to the bill. On this day the Ways and Means Committee

committee, were also put on the stand in support of these
parts of the bill, practically as "Government witnesses," the
arrangements for their appearance having been made,
respectively, by Miss Lenroot and the U.S. Public Health
Service. This concluded the presentation of the case for the

---

had already heard a large number of state health officers in support of the public health sections of the bill. All of these witnesses
gave practically the same testimony, with the result that, after
several hours of such testimony, a member of the committee offered
a motion, which was adopted, that all other witnesses be limited to
five minutes. When Mr. McGrady put Mr. Epstein on the stand, he
overlooked this five-minute rule, but after five minutes the chairman
told Mr. Epstein that his time had expired. Mr. Epstein protested
and a motion was adopted permitting him to continue without regard
to the five-minute rule, but he charged that an attempt was made to
cut short his testimony. On this occasion Mr. Epstein was further
infuriated by being confronted (by Congressman Lewis) with his
testimony in the preceding session of Congress in favor of the
Wagner-Lewis bill, which he now so severely condemned.

Mr. Epstein's testimony was never referred to in the executive
sessions of the Ways and Means Committee and, apparently, made
little impression upon the members of that committee. His even
more extreme opposition to the bill in later testimony before the
Senate Committee on Finance, however, greatly impressed several
of the senators and he was asked by them whether he would be
willing to sit in with the committee in its executive sessions to work
out necessary amendments. By the time the executive sessions were
held, however, no member of the Senate committee even suggested
that Mr. Epstein be called and he was not brought in.

No attempt was made by me to appease Mr. Epstein after his
testimony before the congressional committees and his criticism of
the Committee on Economic Security and the social security bill
became constantly more extreme. At a public meeting at the Brookings Institution in December (before the Committee on Economic
Security had made its report but after the *New York Times* had
forecast its attitude on unemployment compensation), Mr. Epstein
publicly stated that regardless of what the committee and the President might recommend, he could guarantee that Congress would
enact the subsidy plan. He continued to express this belief until
the Senate committee made its report. Thereafter he found everything in the bill to be objectionable except the old age assistance
title, for which he continued to claim credit.

84

bill, no other witnesses appearing at the instance of the Committee on Economic Security. After the first two weeks, Mr. McGrady no longer attended and the committee often had no representative at the hearings other than Wilbur J. Cohen, a junior member of the staff, who attended all hearings as an observer, pursuant to my instructions.

Following the Government witnesses, both congressional committees heard everyone who appeared to testify on the economic security bill. Among these were several members of the advisory council who favored the subsidy plan and increased contribution rates in unemployment compensation (Graham, Kellogg, Miss Hall); a few experts, most of whom took the same position, but some of whom suggested other amendments (Mrs. Burns, Paul Douglas, Tyson, Kulp); Dr. Townsend and several "experts" employed by him (Dr. Doane, Glenn Hudson); supporters of the Lundeen bill (Miss Van Kleeck, Browder, Benjamin); representatives of national women's organizations favoring the bill; representatives of employers' organizations opposed to it; and a considerable miscellany of other witnesses.

Of all these witnesses, those supporting the Townsend plan attracted by far the most public attention. Dr. Townsend and his witnesses did not so much attack the economic security bill as champion their own plan as a substitute for the titles on old age security in the Administration's bill. They were given unlimited time and treated courteously, but the committee members subjected them to a merciless questioning to bring out the weaknesses in their plan. Dr. Townsend and his witnesses made many damaging admissions, which encouraged many members of Congress to come out openly against the Townsend plan. These members were promptly denounced in the *Townsend Weekly*, which charged that Dr. Townsend had been very unfairly treated by the congressional committees.

Dr. Townsend's testimony represented his first appearance before any congressional committee. His appearances before the two congressional committees were widely advertised in advance, attracted the largest audiences of the entire hearings, and received front-page publicity in nearly all daily newspapers. The effect created was that the real issue became the Townsend plan or the economic security bill. Few members of Congress ever thought the Townsend plan a practical possibility, and the testimony given by the Doctor and his witnesses did not strengthen his case with the congressmen. His testimony, however, plus the thousands of letters in support of the Townsend plan with which all congressmen were deluged at this time, caused practically every other feature of the bill and all other sources of opposition to be forgotten.

The supporters of the Lundeen bill more violently attacked the economic security bill, but made a most unfavorable impression. The principal statement in behalf of this group was made by Herbert P. Benjamin, the Secretary of the National Joint Action Committee for Genuine Social Insurance. Mr. Benjamin was very insulting to the House committee and was finally ejected by a policeman. Earl Browder, Executive Secretary of the Communist Party of America, described this measure as the principal method of propaganda of Communists to gain the support of the working people of the country. Miss Mary Van Kleeck, the reputed author of the Lundeen bill, made a much more dignified statement in support of this measure, but the net effect of all of the testimony for this bill was to identify it as a Communist proposal.

Considerably better, but nevertheless, ineffective, was the impression created by the advocates of the subsidy plan for unemployment compensation. The appearance of members of the advisory council and of some "experts" for the subsidy plan, and still more a joint statement[49] for this proposal which was sent to the Senate Finance Committee in February by some thirty people with eminent names, including several former members of the staff of the committee, caused considerable concern in the circles of the Committee on Economic Security. It seemed wisest to make no attempt to reply to this group, lest existing animosities be increased; and this policy proved sound. The members of the congressional committees were not impressed, because they realized that the point at issue in the controversy over the subsidy plan was the greater degree of federal control favored by its advocates; and when it became evident that the real question was whether the Administration's program should be adopted or no social security legislation enacted at all, several of the staunchest advocates of the subsidy plan gave support to the bill.[50]

Organized labor took little part in the congressional hearings. President Green of the A.F. of L. testified as a Government witness before both committees, but was quite critical of the bill. His statement before the Senate committee was a long, carefully prepared memorandum, in which he suggested many amendments. This statement was interpreted in the newspaper dispatches as an attack upon the bill by organized labor. On the next day, before the House committee, he talked offhand and indicated that, while organized labor would like to see the bill amended as he had suggested to the Senate committee, it was for the bill in any event. This accurately reflected the attitude of organized labor. It was far less interested in social security than many other questions, but, while not enthusiastic about the Administra-

49. Published in the *Senate Finance Committee Hearings on the Economic Security Act*, 74th Congress, 1st Session, pp. 1138–40.

50. This was true particularly of President Graham, who had served as chairman of the advisory council, and of President Green of the American Federation of Labor.

tion's program, mildly favored this measure. Friendly relations were maintained by the Committee on Economic Security with Mr. Green and other labor leaders throughout, and, while at first their attitude caused some concern, in the end they let "friendly" senators know that they wanted to see the bill passed, and, particularly, that they did not want to see it weakened by the Clark amendment.[51]

In the hearings there were but few appearances by employers. Henry I. Harriman, President of the United States

51. I have a strong feeling that the positions taken by Mr. Green and other labor leaders at the several stages of the development of the social security legislation were very greatly influenced by factors that had nothing to do with this legislation. When I first consulted Mr. Green he expressed himself as entirely satisfied with the Wagner-Lewis bill, but in the sessions of the advisory council favored the subsidy plan. At that time, organized labor had a grievance against the Administration because of its support of the Automobile Labor Board. When Mr. Green testified in January, the A.F. of L. was strongly fighting the Administration over the prevailing wage amendment to the work relief bill. Later on these disagreements were patched up, and by the spring of 1935 organized labor once more was quite friendly to the Administration. This change, above everything else, was brought about through the Administration's support given the Wagner labor disputes bill. While the President at no stage ever made any public statement on this bill, Secretary Perkins did so at the hearings on this measure. Senator Wagner, moreover, was the author of both the labor disputes bill and the economic security bill. When the controversy over the prevailing wage amendment was at its height, he arranged a conference between a group of progressive senators and the most important leaders of organized labor, including Mr. Green. This conference was not immediately productive of an agreement, and Mr. Green's testimony on the social security bill was given immediately after efforts of Senator Wagner to arrange for a conference by Mr. Green with the President on the prevailing wage amendment had failed. Soon thereafter, however, all differences were ironed out.

Subsequent to the passage of the social security act, the American Federation of Labor included the votes on passage of this measure and on the Clark amendment among the four tests by which it gauged the labor records of the members of Congress in the first session of the 74th Congress.

Chamber of Commerce, suggested amendments, but was generally favorable to the bill; Samuel W. Reybourn, representing the National Retail Dry Goods Association, even more distinctly so.[52] On the other hand, the National Associa-

52. I had several conferences with Mr. Harriman during the fall and again immediately preceding his testimony before the Senate Finance Committee. Mr. Harriman's general attitude was that some legislation on social security was inevitable and that business should not put itself in the position of attempting to block this legislation, but should concentrate its efforts upon getting it into an acceptable form.

The National Retail Dry Goods Association created committees on unemployment insurance and relief in the fall of 1934, which early contacted the Committee on Economic Security. I had conferences both with Mr. Reybourn, chairman of the unemployment insurance committee of this association, and Mr. Kaufman of Pittsburgh, the chairman of the relief committee. The retailers took the position that unemployment insurance was in the interests of the merchants, but wanted the legislation to give benefits immediately to all of the unemployed.

Besides Harriman and Reybourn, Harold W. Story of the Allis-Chalmers Company and M. B. Folsom of the advisory council and the Eastman Kodak Company gave testimony for the bill as Government witnesses, although both suggested amendments. Mr. Folsom impressed the Senate committee so greatly that he was asked whether he would be willing to confer with the committee in its executive session. In the end, however, he was not called in because Chairman Harrison did not think it advisable to bring in any outsiders. Mr. Folsom's testimony, however, was frequently quoted by senators in the executive sessions.

The Business Advisory and Planning Council of the (U.S.) Department of Commerce organized a Committee on Industrial Relations about the time the Committee on Economic Security was created. This committee in November, 1934, prepared a confidential "Preliminary Memorandum on Unemployment Insurance," which was, unofficially, delivered to me to be presented informally to the Committee on Economic Security. One member of the committee (Col. Robert G. Elbert) published this confidential memorandum and a criticism thereof in book form, under the title *Unemployment and Relief* (Farrar S. Rinehart, 1935). This caused some embarrassment to the committee, and it thereafter, apparently, decided to function through members of the Business Advisory and Planning Council who were employer members of the Advisory Council on Economic

tion of Manufacturers, the Illinois Manufacturers' Association, and the Ohio Manufacturers' Association violently attacked the bill. When the congressional hearings were held, employers generally knew too little about the bill to take any very decided stand upon it. Later, they were stirred up by opponents of the measure and sent many protests, by letters and telegrams, to their members of Congress.

The opponents of the economic security bill concentrated upon the Senate committee, many of them not even taking the trouble to appear before the House committee. This was in accord with the belief widely entertained that the real test of the strength of the bill would come in the Senate committee, it being assumed that the Administration controlled the House committee. This attitude helped the bill. Actually, the members of the Senate, as a group, manifested much less interest in this legislation than did the members of the House committee. By the time the opponents were heard, the attendance of the senators was quite slim, and their arguments failed to create much of an impression.

The hearings of the Ways and Means Committee lasted nearly three weeks, from January 21 to February 12. Hearings were held both mornings and afternoons, and in the early stages practically all members of the committee were in attendance continuously. In the Senate the hearings were conducted more leisurely, extending from January 22 to

Security (Teagle, Leeds, Swope). After the Committee on Economic Security made its report (which was not entirely satisfactory to this group), the question of an appearance before the congressional committees was discussed, but a negative decision was reached. Later (under date of April 10, 1935), however, the Committee on Social Legislation of the Business Advisory and Planning Council (which was either the successor of the Committee on Industrial Relations, referred to in this paragraph, or had many overlapping members) made a report in which it urged numerous changes in the unemployment insurance sections of the social security bill. This was transmitted to the President and given publicity through the newspapers, but attracted little attention in Congress.

February 20. These hearings were held only in the forenoon, and after the first few meetings were not attended very strongly.[53] Both committees were interested principally in old age security, particularly old age assistance. Much of the testimony related to other parts of the bill, but did not interest the members very much. Summing up the hearings, it may be said that they lasted longer than expected and disclosed strong opposition to the bill, but left every hope for reasonably prompt passage.

Consideration by the Ways and Means Committee and the Redrafting of the Bill

The Ways and Means Committee began executive sessions on the economic security bill immediately after the conclusions of its hearings. It did not complete its consideration of the bill, however, until the first days in April. During much of the intervening time it met every day in an attempt to get this bill out for action at an early date. Finally, in the middle of March, it sidetracked this bill for the bonus measure and did not come back to it until the latter bill was out of the House. All told, the House Ways and Means Committee held at least twenty executive sessions of the entire committee on the bill, and literally went over every word of the measure. At various times reference to a subcommittee or subcommittees was suggested, but was strongly resisted by the chairman. Near the end, however, the old age insurance titles were referred to a subcommittee (headed by Congressman Vinson) and this, perhaps, hastened final disposition. Aside from this one instance, however, the committee made no use of subcommittees on this measure, leaving twenty-five members to decide details.

53. Practically all members of the Senate Finance Committee served also on other committees which were conducting other hearings simultaneously. The members, consequently had to "flit" in and out, and while there generally was a respectable attendance, only the chairman really sat through all of the hearings.

The long delay which resulted at this stage, I believe, was due principally to the following factors:

1. *Redrafting of the Bill by the Chief Draftsman of the House, Mr. Beaman.* The Ways and Means Committee always works very closely with the bill draftsmen of the House. The leaders of this committee, as well as Mr. Beaman, did not like it that they had not been consulted in advance; moreover, it was very evident that the bill would have to be redrafted in certain respects. Chairman Doughton, early during the hearings, consequently, instructed Mr. Beaman to undertake this work of redrafting the bill in conjunction with Mr. Eliot, Counsel of the Committee on Economic Security.

Mr. Beaman worked exceedingly deliberately, spending hours in conference with his staff and Mr. Eliot over particular phrases. Only after he had completed redrafting the several titles of the bill did the Ways and Means Committee begin considering them.

Mr. Beaman attended all the executive sessions of the Ways and Means Committee[54] and greatly influenced its action. More than any other individual, he was responsible for the language in which the bill was finally put. Through his work he undoubtedly improved the measure, particularly

54. Mr. Eliot also attended all sessions, and I did so when I was in Washington. When I could not be there, Dr. Joseph P. Harris took my place. Dr. Harris and I took part in the discussions only when asked to do so by the committee. Eliot and Beaman volunteered information frequently, particularly Beaman. The points which he raised were generally technical, but not infrequently involved matters of policy.

In addition to those already mentioned, Mr. Parker and Mr. Stamm of the Joint Committee on Taxation, and either Mr. Erb or Mr. Wilcox of the legal division of the Treasury Department attended most of the executive sessions of the Ways and Means Committee and participated, to a minor degree, in its deliberations. Wilbur J. Cohen, my personal research assistant, also attended all of the executive sessions of both congressional committees.

with respect to the likelihood of its being held constitutional, but his deliberateness was a major factor in the long delay in the Ways and Means Committee, and his generally unfavorable comments on the policies of the bill strengthened the position of the members of the committee who did not like the measure.

2. *The Attitude of a Majority of the Members of the Ways and Means Committee.* Few of the members of the Ways and Means Committee were sympathetic with the economic security bill. An outstanding exception was Congressman Lewis, who, however, was without much influence. Congressmen Brooks and Dingell likewise were favorable to the measure, but were among the younger members. Congressmen Cooper, McCormack, and Woodruff were very sympathetic with the bill. I doubt whether many other members would have supported the measure but for the fact that it had the endorsement of the President. Chairman Doughton and Congressmen Hill, Vinson, Cooper, and McCormack, who were, at all odds, the most important members of the committee, were anxious to carry out the President's wishes. Some other members were hostile from the beginning, particularly Congressmen Lamneck and Boehne, both Democrats. The minority members at first seemed quite friendly, but seemed to feel that they necessarily had to oppose the Administration's program, at least in some respects.

It was over the old age insurance provisions that the most serious contest developed within the committee. About a week before the committee's report, it seemed probable that the old age insurance titles would be completely stricken from the bill. Congressman Fuller canvassed the members in favor of such a move, and it was reported that he had a majority of one in his favor. An agreement was then made by Congressman Vinson with some of the doubtful members, under which the principal Administration leaders supported a motion to eliminate the title on voluntary annuities, while these doubtful members agreed to support the compulsory old age insurance title. Thereupon, the voluntary insurance title was stricken out almost unanimously, while the compulsory insurance title received a majority vote of three or four.

In the final vote on the bill, all Democratic members of the Ways and Means Committee voted in favor of recommending passage with the exception of Congressman Lamneck (who was absent on account of illness, but was known to be irreconcilably opposed to the bill). None of the Republican members voted for the bill, but they made a minority report in which they put themselves on record as favoring the assistance provisions and as being willing to give the unemployment insurance titles a trial, but expressed dissent from compulsory old age insurance.

3. *Failure of Any Decisive Leadership in Support of the Bill.* The President, at this time, apparently deemed it advisable to avoid all appearance of attempting to dictate to Congress.[55] In connection with the economic security bill, he insisted that this bill should come before Congress like any ordinary measure. In his message he indicated that he did not expect Congress to merely act as a rubber stamp. When the Ways and Means Committee got into the consideration of the bill in executive sessions, the Administration members went to the President to ask him, point blank, how much of the bill he insisted upon having passed. The President told these members that he believed that all parts of the bill should be passed, but that he did not wish to dictate details.

55. The President's prestige at this time had been somewhat weakened by the refusal of the Senate to ratify the treaty for the World Court and the passage of the bonus bill over the President's opposition, and his inability to get prompt action on the work relief bill. Very evidently, the President at this stage was trying to leave Congress pretty much to its own devices, to avoid criticisms that he was attempting to dictate and to convince the congressional leaders that they could do nothing without him.

Somewhat later the President was again consulted by these members and advised that the old age insurance provisions could not be passed. The President then insisted that this was the most important part of the bill and very definitely gave these Administration leaders to understand that all essential parts of the measure must remain intact. It is my belief that the President's insistence at this stage saved the old age insurance titles and possibly also the unemployment insurance titles; but this did not occur until late in March.

Plus the President's desire not to interfere with the congressional consideration of the economic security bill, Chairman Doughton's fairness operated to slow action. The executive sessions were little more than round-table meetings. Several members often talked at once, motions made were not even put to a vote; day after day there was postponement of action. Chairman Doughton was personally very popular with the members, and this popularity helped finally to carry the bill, but his method of conducting the executive sessions, accounted for some of the delay.[56]

4. The Strength of the Townsend Movement. The members of the House of Representatives at all times took the Townsend movement much more seriously than did the senators. The thousands of letters which the members received in support of this plan worried them greatly. With the exception of probably not more than a half dozen members, all

56. There was a great contrast in this respect between Congressman Doughton and Senator Harrison. I attribute favorable action in the Senate Finance Committee very largely to the exceptionally able handling of the committee by Chairman Harrison. It is my belief that, if it had been possible to get votes in the Ways and Means Committee on the important points in controversy soon after the conclusions of the hearings, the votes would have been very nearly unanimous in favor of the provisions of the bill. Later on the delays which occurred were not altogether unfavorable, as there was a real chance in March that the bill would be badly mutilated. As I see it, the credit for the final favorable result belonged to Congressman Vinson and, above all others, to the President.

felt that the Townsend plan was utterly impossible; at the same time they hesitated to vote against it. The Townsend movement had the effect of taking away from the economic security bill its strongest natural support—that of the old people. As the situation developed, the congressmen could not get any credit through voting for old age assistance on the moderate basis provided for in the economic security bill, while they could not vote for the Townsend plan because they felt it would wreck the country.

5. *Increasing Opposition to the Bill from Many Sources.* Practically all of the letters which the members of Congress received on the economic security bill were critical or hostile. This included not only the thousands of letters from the Townsendites but many from businessmen who did not like the taxes proposed in the bill. They also included letters from many supporters of social insurance who expressed agreement with the purposes of the bill but criticized its provisions. The net impression created by this correspondence was that there was serious opposition to the bill and no real support.

This situation finally aroused the Committee on Economic Security and the President to action. Secretary Perkins and Dr. Altmeyer originally did not think that there would be any serious trouble in getting the bill through the House of Representatives.[57] When the consideration in the executive session of the Ways and Means Committee dragged on indefinitely, however, they realized that the situation was really critical. Secretary Perkins then got in touch with a number of people who she felt could be relied upon to give wholehearted support to the bill and also urged the President to make it clear to the congressional leaders that he really wanted the bill to be passed substantially as intro-

57. This was also the view of the President, who stated that the real fight would come in the Senate and that it did not matter much what amendments the House attached to the bill.

duced. The supporters of the bill called together by the secretary secured some fifty signatures of prominent people to a public letter addressed to the Ways and Means Committee urging prompt passage of the bill as it stood and also initiated something of a campaign to get some people to urge their members of Congress to support the bill;[58] and the President, as already recited, told the Administration leaders of the Ways and Means Committee that he considered every part of the original bill to be essential. This activity in support of the bill came at the most critical time and marked a distinct turning point in the history of the measure.

The Ways and Means Committee concluded its work with an entirely new bill. This bill did not differ so very greatly from the original measure in content, but differed greatly in arrangement and language. The bill was given a new number and even a different general title. Until then it had been the "Economic Security Act"; now it became the "Social Security Act." This measure was introduced as a

58. A conference was held in the offices of the Secretary of Labor, in which the following, and perhaps some others, were present: Miss Grace Abbott, Miss Lenroot, Father O'Grady, Frank Bane, John B. Andrews, and Dr. Altmeyer. (I was not in Washington at the time and did not participate in the conference.) A public statement was prepared in which the signers stated that, while not in agreement on every detail, they all were hopeful that Congress would promptly pass the economic security bill substantially as introduced. This was signed by many leading liberals of great prominence and was given wide publicity through the newspapers. At the same time organizations friendly to the social security program (women's organizations, the Eagles, and some others) were apprized of the need for showing Congress that this program had some real support. The American Public Welfare Association contributed money to employ Dr. John B. Andrews to organize support for the economic security bill. Personal lobbying with members in behalf of the bill was done by Assistant Secretary McGrady, Mr. Bane, Dr. Andrew, and Father O'Grady. The total amount of work of this character was not very great at this stage or any other, but I believe that it was very helpful.

committee bill and took the place of the prior Doughton and Lewis bills.

The committee's favorable report was formally filed on April 5. The first part of this report, presenting an argument in support of the bill, was largely written by myself, with assistance from Dr. Harris; the second part, which explained in detail the several provisions of the bill, by Messrs. Beaman and Eliot.

Debate in the House

Consideration of the social security bill began in the House on April 11. A special rule for the consideration of the bill was reported by the House Rules Committee, but this rule left the bill wide open to amendment. Very few important bills in recent years have been considered under such a wide-open rule. It was feared by the supporters of the bill that this would mean that it would leave the House in almost unrecognizable form. The Ways and Means Committee had asked for a rule of the usual type, barring or limiting votes on amendments. The Rules Committee turned down this request, apparently because it did not wish to offend the Townsendites. As it developed, this wide-open rule did not in any manner prove a handicap. It stopped much of the criticism that the bill was being railroaded through Congress, while the House leaders demonstrated that they could control their supporters without a restrictive rule.[59]

The debate in the House lasted until April 19. Approximately fifty amendments were offered, but none of them came even close to adoption. Difficulty had been anticipated over an amendment to substitute the Townsend plan for

59. The House leaders passed the word around that they wanted all amendments killed, and some of them held meetings with their own delegations to get them committed to such an attitude. Among others, this was done by Chairman Doughton with the North Carolina delegation.

98

the old age security provision in the bill and still more over amendments to place the entire cost of old age assistance on the federal government and to increase the maximum grants for this purpose.[60] The latter amendment (presented in the form of a proposal to increase the old age assistance grants to $50 per month and to have the federal government pay the entire costs) received the largest vote of any proposed amendment, but was defeated by a large majority. Amendments to substitute the Townsend plan and the Lundeen bill for the committee bill both mustered in the neighborhood of fifty votes, and most of those voting for these proposals were opposed to any sort of social security legislation rather than genuine supporters of these radical measures.[61]

Final passage came on April 19 by a vote of Yeas 371, Nays 33. The minority was composed of a handful of ardent supporters of the Townsend plan or the Lundeen bill, plus a somewhat larger number of conservatives who were opposed to all social security legislation.

Consideration in the Senate Committee

At the time when the social security bill passed the House, the Senate Finance Committee was busy with the bonus and tax bills. It did not take up the social security bill until it was through with these two measures. This was

60. This amendment was offered by Congresswoman Greenway of Arizona, a close friend to Mrs. Roosevelt, who went directly to the President to urge his approval of the amendment. The President's refusal to do so was a major factor in the defeat of the amendment.

61. The vote on the Townsend plan amendment was not taken by roll call, but by division. The members voting for the amendment, however, were listed in the newspapers and in the *Townsend Weekly*. The great majority of members who voted for the Townsend plan were conservative Republicans who opposed the entire social security bill. The names of the persons supporting the Lundeen bill were not reported, but again most of them were opponents of the social security bill, rather than genuine supporters of the Lundeen bill.

during the first days in May, approximately two and a half months after the committee had completed its hearings on the original bill.

From the first it was realized that the Senate Finance Committee would probably constitute the most serious obstacle to the enactment of the social security bill. A very large percentage of the members of this committee were from south of the Mason and Dixon Line, and several of the members were among the most conservative of all senators. To add to the difficulties, the United States Supreme Court on May 6, a few days after the Senate Finance Committee began executive sessions on the social security bill, held unconstitutional the Railroad Retirement Act. Language used in this decision seemed to apply also to the old age insurance provisions of the social security bill. Considerable discussion developed in the committee over the effect of this decision and the Attorney General was asked an opinion on the point. This opinion was presented by Assistant Solicitor General McLean, and was to the effect that the decision did not necessarily render any part of the social security bill unconstitutional. This, however, did not satisfy some members of the committee, who centered their attack on the pending bill on the unconstitutionality of the measure.

The executive sessions of the Senate Finance Committee were conducted much like those of the House Ways and Means Committee, but in a more formal and orderly manner. The draftsmen of both the House and Senate (Mr. Beaman and Mr. Boots), Mr. Parker and Mr. Stam of the Joint Committee on Taxation, Mr. Erb and often Mr. Wilcox of the office of the Counsel of the Treasury, Mr. Eliot, I, and sometimes still other representatives of the Committee on Economic Security, attended all sessions. At the first meeting Secretary Perkins was heard on amendments desired by the Committee on Economic Security. The bill as

100

it passed the House was very unsatisfactory to the committee. On March 15, when the House bill was practically in final form but had not been approved by the committee, Secretary Perkins presented to the President a memorandum outlining certain amendments which the Committee on Economic Security deemed very important and urged him to suggest to the leaders of the Ways and Means Committee that these amendments must be included in the bill. A little later, amendments in legislative form were prepared by Mr. Eliot and presented by him and myself to Professor Moley, to be taken to the President.[62] Later, after the House had passed the bill, another memorandum was prepared which Secretary Perkins took to the President on April 28. In this memorandum the President was urged to exert his influence in favor of the following amendments:[63]

1. To restore to the states the right to have either an individual employer account or pooled-fund type of unemployment compensation law. (This was something the President himself was very insistent upon.)

2. To put the Social Security Board back into the Department of Labor.

3. To make retirement from regular employment a condition of receiving old age pensions.

4. To place the administration of the aid for dependent children in the Children's Bureau.

5. To restore the provisions of the original bill for selection on a merit basis of personnel concerned with the administration of the social security program in the states.

62. It is my belief that the President never presented these amendments to the leaders of the Ways and Means Committee, although he told them orally that he wanted all of the essential provisions of the original bill preserved.

63. Whether the President discussed these amendments (with all of which he agreed) with the leaders of the Senate Finance Committee, I do not know, but the first three of the above suggestions were included in the amendments approved by the committee.

These same amendments were presented by Secretary Perkins to the Senate Finance Committee in her appearance in its executive sessions. Thereafter, representatives of the Treasury Department, the Post Office Department, the Budget Bureau, and Governor Winship of Puerto Rico were heard by the committee and suggested minor amendments. Only after these witnesses had been heard did the committee begin its own discussions of the bill. Unlike the proceedings in the executive sessions of the House Ways and Means Committee, a complete stenographic record was kept of all statements made in the executive sessions of the Senate Finance Committee and printed for the confidential use of the members.

The major subjects which provoked controversy in the Senate Finance Committee were the compulsory old age insurance plan, voluntary old age annuities, the Clark amendment relating to industrial pensions, and the relation of the Social Security Board to the Department of Labor. The latter was disposed of by an amendment which placed the Social Security Board within the Department of Labor, but deprived the Secretary of Labor of control over the personnel of the Board.[64] The restoration of voluntary annuities was urged before the committee in a speech by Congressman Lewis, but was strongly opposed by Senator Lonergan. A motion to put voluntary annuities back into the bill carried by one vote, at a time when there was a slim attendance. The chairman cast the deciding vote, but immediately thereafter reassured Senator Lonergan that he would not object if the Senate did not adopt this amend-

64. While the Senate Finance Committee agreed to this amendment, I always felt that it did so expecting to recede in conference. Chairman Harrison himself felt rather edgewise toward Secretary Perkins and there were but few members of the committee who were really desirous to have the Department of Labor control the Social Security Board.

ment. The question whether a compulsory old age insurance provision should remain in the bill was one on which the outcome was most doubtful. Had Chairman Harrison allowed this question to come to a vote earlier than it did, I feel quite sure that Title II would have gone out of the bill. When the vote finally came, it occurred under the most favorable circumstances possible[65] and the motion to strike out title II lost by a substantial majority. The Clark amendment was defeated more narrowly, failing of adoption by a tie vote and with several members absent who might have voted for this amendment.

After disposition of these most controversial matters, the chairman got the committee, without a roll-call vote, to

65. On the evening preceding this vote, Senator King, who throughout was personally very friendly to me, talked to me about the bill. He indicated that he could not see how he could support either the old age insurance or the unemployment compensation titles. He finally said that he would vote for unemployment compensation, if I would prepare an argument for him which he might use in opposing old age insurance. I took him up and prepared the best argument I knew how against old age insurance and sent this to Senator King, within a few hours after he made his request.

The next day, at the final executive session of the Senate Finance Committee, Senator King read my argument. Introductory remarks which he made led the members of the committee to believe that this argument had been written by Henry E. Jackson, President of the Social Engineering Institute of New York City, an opponent of compulsory old age insurance, who was often quoted by Senator King. After the conclusion of Senator King's statement, without any connivance on my part, I was called on to present the argument for old age insurance. I had not anticipated this, but I had pretty well in mind what I thought was the only possible argument which might win enough support to carry the day in the Senate. This was a frank acknowledgement of the difficulties certain to be encountered in old age insurance, but with an emphasis upon the fact that the probable alternative was a modified Townsend plan. Chairman Harrison then, immediately after my speech, put the question to a vote and every member of the committee who was considered doubtful voted for old age insurance.

agree to immediately report the bill for passage. Throughout the consideration of the bill in the Senate Finance Committee, Chairman Harrison displayed remarkable ability in getting what he wanted. When motions were offered and he felt uncertain how they would go, he managed to put over the vote to a subsequent meeting. Amendments which he favored he declared adopted, unless there was prompt objection. He held back the vote on the most controversial subjects until he felt sure of the vote. On the final day, when the most important votes were taken, he held proxies from Senator Couzens, the ranking minority member, who was then seriously ill, and from Senator Walsh. He carried with him Senators Lonergan, Guffey, and Gerry, whose votes were doubtful. Senators Byrd and Bailey, who were definitely hostile, were absent, without giving proxies to anyone. With a less adroit chairman, the social security bill would probably have emerged from the Senate committee in a very unsatisfactory form, if indeed a favorable report could have been secured. As it was, the majority of amendments reported were distinctly improvements and in accord with the desires of the Committee on Economic Security.

The report of the Senate Finance Committee was prepared much as was the House report. I wrote the first part of this report, revising completely the argument for the bill which was included in the House report. The second part, stating in technical language the provisions of the bill, section by section, followed closely the corresponding report of the House, with such changes as were necessitated by the Senate amendments. The members of the committee who opposed the bill did not bother to write a minority report. The report in favor of passage was filed in the Senate on May 20, a few days after the Finance Committee had finished with the measure.

Senate Debate

There was another delay of more than three weeks before the Senate took up the social security bill. This was due to the fact that other bills had precedence on the calendar and that Senator Long staged his record filibuster just before the social security bill was scheduled to be brought up. Debate on this bill began on June 14 and continued on the 15, 17, 18, and 19. The defense of the measure fell principally to Senators Harrison, Wagner, La Follette, Barkley, and Costigan. Attacks upon the bill were made by Senators Hastings, Hale, King, George, and Long. Most of the debate concerned the old age insurance provisions, particularly the Clark amendment.

All of the amendments recommended by the committee were adopted without much discussion or a roll-call vote, except the amendment relating to voluntary annuities. This was kept out of the blanket motion of Senator Harrison for the adoption of committee amendments. Senator Lonergan moved that this amendment be rejected and this motion prevailed, without objection from anyone except Senator Costigan.

The real fight in the Senate concerned the Clark amendment. The debate on this amendment was at times quite bitter. Senator Clark assailed the "experts" who, he stated, outnumbered the senators in the executive sessions of the Senate Finance Committee and some of whom were on the Senate floor.[66] Senators La Follette and Barkley replied in kind, charging that the promoter of the Clark amendment[67] was interested solely in the commissions which he could get

66. This was a reference to Mr. Calhoun, majority expert of the Senate Finance Committee, and to Mr. Eliot and myself. At the request of Chairman Harrison, we occupied seats on the floor to supply information to the supporters of the bill as needed.

67. Mr. Walter Forster, of Towers, Perrin, Forster, & Crosby, Inc., Philadelphia, insurance counselors and brokers.

through selling industrial pension plans. A vast amount of lobbying was carried on in connection with this amendment.[68] Both organized labor and the Administration definitely opposed this amendment, but it was adopted, by a vote of 51 to 35, on June 19.

After the Clark amendment was disposed of, another very damaging amendment, the Russell amendment, was approved, practically without any contest. This amendment provided that states which were prevented from complying with the conditions for federal aid for old age assistance by reason of provisions in their constitutions or because their legislatures were not in session should receive aid until July 1, 1937, without any requirement of matching.

Thereafter, on the same day, the Senate passed the social security bill, 77 to 6, the minority being composed of five conservative Republicans and Senator Moore of New Jersey. Senators Byrd and Gore were paired against the bill and Senator Tydings voted "present." Senators King, George, and Long, who had attacked the bill on the floor voted for it on passage.

Conference between the Houses

The amendments which the Senate attached to the social security bill were rejected as a matter of form when they came up in the House. This was a preliminary to the appoint-

68. Senator Clark and Congressman Boehne worked on the Senate floor itself to get members committed to the amendment. Messrs. Forster, Hamilton, and Horlick (the latter two representing the Equitable Life Assurance Society) did a vast amount of lobbying in the anterooms. On the other side, the White House was trying to get the senators committed against adoption of the amendment. Former Congressman West and Vice-President Garner spoke to many senators urging them to vote against the Clark amendment. In the debate most of the Administration leaders, particularly Senators Robinson and Harrison, strongly opposed the amendment. On the other hand, nearly all Republicans favored the amendment, as did half the Democrats.

ment of a Committee on Conference, the selection of which was completed on June 20. Pursuant to the usual practice governing the selection of conference committees, the Senate conferees were Senators Harrison, King, and George, Democrats; Keyes, Republican; and La Follette, Progressive.[69] The House conferees were Congressmen Doughton, Hill, and Cullen, Democrats; Treadway and Bacharach, Republicans. This was a very unfortunate committee due to the fact that a majority of the Senate conferees were really opposed to the bill.[70]

The Conference Committee did not begin consideration of the bill for nearly ten days and then proceeded only very slowly. From the first it seemed probable that there would be no very great difficulty in securing an agreement on all amendments except the Clark amendment, but on this amendment there appeared to be no possibility of compromise. When I left for Europe on July 6, no agreement had been reached, and such an agreement was, in fact, not arrived at until August. By the middle of July, all other matters in conference except the Clark amendment had been adjusted, but no agreement had been reached on this amendment. On July 16, both conference committees made reports to their respective houses, recommending adoption of the agreement reached on all amendments other than the Clark amendment and asking for further instructions relative to this amendment. On July 17, both the Senate and the

69. Senator La Follette was put on the conference committee because Senator Couzens, the ranking minority member, was seriously ill. Senator La Follette was the next minority member in rank.

70. As has been stated, Senators King and George talked against the bill in the Senate Finance Committee and while it was on the floor of the Senate. Had they voted as they talked, Senators Walsh and Barkley would have been the Democratic Senate conferees in addition to Senator Harrison. Because they voted for the bill on final passage, however, they secured places on the Conference Committee, although opposed to the old age insurance title of the bill.

House accepted the conference reports and each house instructed its conferees to adhere to their position on the Clark amendment.

The conference committee then intructed the legislative draftsmen and Mr. Eliot to work out an amendment, in conjunction with attorneys representing the promoters of the Clark amendment, accomplishing the same purpose but in a constitutional manner. Several weeks were devoted to trying to work out such a new amendment, but in the end all of the draftsmen made a written statement to the conferees that a much longer time was required to work out this amendment than the probable length of the Congressional session. The conferees then reached an agreement, under which the social security bill was recommended for passage without the Clark amendment, but with the understanding that a special committee of the two houses would be appointed to prepare a suitable amendment, embodying the essence of the Clark amendment, to be presented to Congress at its next session.

The House accepted the conference report on August 8, the Senate on August 9, in both instances without a roll-call vote. The President signed the measure on August 14, 1935, and the Social Security Act became law on that day.

Edwin E. Witte, Frances Perkins, and Frank P. Graham (standing) at the opening of the National Conference on Economic Security, November 14, 1934.

President Franklin D. Roosevelt signing the social security bill, August 14, 1935. Grouped about the President, left to right, are: Chairman Robert L. Doughton of the House Ways and Means Committee; Congressman Frank H. Buck (D—Calif.); Senator Robert F. Wagner (D—New York); Senator Robert M. La Follette, Jr. (Prog—Wis.); Senator Augustine Lonergan (D—Conn.); Secretary of Labor Frances Perkins; Senator William H. King (D—Utah); Congressman David J. Lewis (D—Md.); and Senator Joseph F. Guffey (D—Penn.).

PART II

Provisions
of the
Social Security
Act

UNEMPLOYMENT COMPENSATION

Early Developments

Having reviewed the history of the Social Security Act generally, it is appropriate to discuss the development of the several parts of the act in some detail.

Unemployment compensation was regarded by the Committee on Economic Security and its staff as the most important part of the entire legislation. In Congress and on the part of the general public, however, there was far less interest in this subject than in old age assistance.

The high points of the development of the unemployment compensation provisions of the original social security bill have already been recited. This story begins with the President's special message on June 8, 1934. In this message, besides promising legislation on the subject, the President indicated that he favored a plan providing for a maximum of coöperation between the states and the federal government, leaving to the states "a large portion of the cost of management" and to the federal government "the responsibility of investing, maintaining and safeguarding the funds constituting the necessary insurance reserves." He further stated that he believed "that the funds necessary to provide this insurance should be raised by contribution rather than by an increase in general taxation" and that unemployment insurance should be set up in such a way as to encourage the stabilization of employment.

I entered upon my work as executive director of the Committee on Economic Security in the fixed belief that these statements of the President constituted definite instructions to the committee. I found that this was also the view of the chairman of the committee, Secretary Perkins, and of Dr. Altmeyer, the chairman of the technical board; and this view was strengthened by the conference which we had with the President late in August.

When the technical board was organized, I learned that many of its members had a very different conception of the work to be done. Their view was that nothing should be regarded as decided and that our major task was to determine upon the best policies to be recommended. I then realized that the committee itself would have to decide the major questions of policy and hoped that it might do so in connection with its consideration of the preliminary report of the staff.

In this preliminary report, Dr. Bryce Stewart outlined a plan for a national system of unemployment insurance, with employer, employee, and governmental contributions administered exclusively by the federal government, but with provisions under which entire industries and, perhaps, large single employers might have their own funds. On my part, I recommended a coöperative federal-state system, developed as suggested in the President's message of June 8.

The portions of the preliminary report dealing with unemployment compensation were referred to the Committee on Unemployment Insurance of the technical board. That committee, after meeting with Dr. Stewart and Mr. Murray, on September 26, made a report to the executive committee of the technical board, in favor of a national plan, but differing in details from some of the specific recommendations made by Dr. Stewart.[71] The executive committee, after ex-

71. The complete report of this committee made to the executive committee of the technical board was as follows:

The committee considered only the major issues involved in the structure of a plan of unemployment insurance, feeling that the more detailed phases of plan structure would have to wait upon decision in the more fundamental points. The recommendations of the committee are as follows:

(1) The Federal Goverment should establish a national system and administer the plan in preference to the Wagner-Lewis procedure or any procedure involving state administration. (Unanimous)

(2) In the first instance, at least all contributions should be pooled. (Unanimous)

tended discussion, adopted the following statement on unemployment compensation, which was included in its preliminary report presented to the Committee on Economic Security at its meeting on October 1:

Compulsory Unemployment Insurance. On this subject the present trend of thought (subject to change) of the Board runs along the following lines:

(*a*) Unemployment insurance is an essential measure for the economic security of the most stable part of our industrial population, but is not a complete, all sufficient solution of the problem.

(*b*) Unemployment insurance should be strictly contractual, divorced from any means test. Unemployment insurance funds should not be used for relief or any other purposes other than the payment of ordinary benefits.

(*c*) Unemployment insurance should be supported by contributions from the employers and probably also from the employees. There should be no public contributions.

(*d*) All contributions should at the outset be pooled in a single fund but there should be further exploration of the advisability of permitting "contracting out" by separate industrial and

---

(3) *Industries should be allowed to contract out and to establish approved industrial schemes. (One member dissenting)*

(4) *House funds should not be permitted. (1 Dissent; 1 Partial Dissent)*

(5) *If there is any breakdown of the general pooled fund into separate funds, a proportion of all contributions should be set aside in a national reinsurance fund to guarantee the ordinary benefits contracted for by the separate funds. (Unanimous)*

(6) *Provision should be made in emergency unemployment situations for the payment of extended benefits from Federal government funds to workers who have exhausted their right to ordinary benefit. (One vote reserved)*

(7) *Contributions from employers and employees to unemployment insurance should in no case be utilized to finance public works. (Unanimous)*

(8) *It is fundamental to the success of a plan of unemployment insurance that both employers and employees should contribute. (Unanimous)*

house funds under restrictions adequately safeguarding the employees.

(e) Benefits should be paid in cash for a limited period only, in proportion to the claimant's period of employment, and should be sufficient to support the family while being paid.

(f) If constitutional, a nationally administered system of unemployment insurance is to be preferred to a state system, but the Committee should be satisfied that a nationally administered system is constitutional before commitments in favor of such a system are made to the public.

(g) If unemployment insurance is to be developed under a system of state administration or if industrial or house funds are permitted, a portion of all contributions should be set aside in a national reinsurance fund to guarantee payment of the contractual benefits from the separate funds.

The Committee on Economic Security, at its meeting on October 1, took no action on any of the tentative recommendations, except to express approval of the scope of the studies which were being made and to refer all subjects back to the technical board and the staff for further study. At this meeting, it was informally agreed that the committee would hold one or more evening meetings to discuss the recommendations it should make on unemployment compensation, as soon as the staff and the technical board had reached more definite decisions. No such meeting was held until November 9, due to the fact that the technical board was not prepared until then to make further recommendations. Throughout October and the early part of November the members of the staff working on unemployment insurance and other interested staff members and the technical board wrestled with this subject. Meetings were held at least once each week, which were participated in by the executive committee and the unemployment insurance committee of the technical board and all major staff members. These conferences developed wide differences of opinion, not only over detail but also over the objectives of unemployment compensation. These differences concerned not merely the fundamental question of an exclusive federal system of unemployment compensation versus a federal-state system, but such matters as the relation of unemployment compensation to relief and public employment, the devices which might be included in the unemployment compensation legislation to promote the regularization of employment, and possible methods of administering an exclusively federal system. As the conferences continued, it became more and more evident that nothing like unanimous agreement was possible on any of these issues either among the staff members or on the technical board.

The major question of the type of the federal legislation to be recommended was envisaged originally in terms of an exclusively federal system or something akin to the Wagner-Lewis bill of the previous session of Congress, under which the federal govenment would levy a tax on employers throughout the country against which an offset would be allowed for payments made under state unemployment compensation acts meeting a few standards prescribed in the federal law. In the course of the conferences of the staff and the technical board during the month of October, there was advanced[72] an alternative proposal for a federal-state coöperative plan, which came to be called the "subsidy plan." This plan was, in essence, that the amount of the revenues collected through the federal tax from employers in each state be returned to that state to be used for unemployment compensation purposes, subject to the state's compliance with standards to be prescribed by the federal government.

72. I believe that this plan was first suggested casually by Mr. Emerson Ross of the staff of the committee and the F.E.R.A. It seemed to me a possible compromise between the advocates of a national system and the Wagner-Lewis bill, and so I urged that it be given serious consideration.

This subsidy plan satisfied the condition, which everyone understood the President would insist upon, that all unemployment compensation funds be deposited in the federal reserve banks or the United States Treasury, so that their investment and liquidation could be controlled by the same governmental agency which was responsible for the credit policies of the government. It was also regarded as a method which could more easily be converted into an exclusively federal system than one in which unemployment compensation funds are collected by the states. Further, it was thought to allow of more federal regulation than would be possible under the offset method of the Wagner-Lewis bill. For these reasons, the subsidy plan was favored as a sort of second choice by members of the staff whose first choice was an exclusively federal system (Bryce Stewart, Mrs. Armstrong, J. Douglas Brown, Merrill G. Murray). On the other hand, it was not acceptable to the members of the staff or the technical board who felt that it was impossible, without actual experience, to prescribe uniform provisions for unemployment compensation which would be reasonably acceptable.[73] There were general memoranda by Messrs. Stewart, Murray, Shipman, and Harris, and by Mrs. Armstrong on the respective advantages of these several plans; and a somewhat detailed outline of a possible administrative procedure in the collection of a federal tax for unemployment insurance purposes by Messrs. Stewart and Murray.

While the staff and the technical board were considering and debating these issues, interested outsiders urged the desirability for an early definite announcement whether an exclusively federal system or a coöperative federal-state system would be recommended by the Administration. This

73. In connection with the conferences of the staff and the technical board, numerous memoranda were prepared on many different aspects of the problems raised under each type of federal law. There were memoranda on the constitutionality of each type of unemployment insurance bill by Mr. Eliot.

was most strongly urged by Dr. John B. Andrews, the secretary of the American Association for Labor Legislation, and by Abraham Epstein, the secretary of the American Association for Social Security, both of whom complained that the uncertainty as to what the Administration would recommend was seriously handicapping their organizations in planning their legislative campaigns for 1935. Further, there were a half-dozen state interim legislative committees which were pressing the committee for advance information on what it was likely to recommend, and, above all, December 1 was rapidly approaching, by which time the committee had to complete its report to the President.

In this situation, the technical board simply had to make a decision on at least the major question of the type of federal legislation to be recommended. It finally did so, after several long executive sessions early in November. The Unemployment Insurance Committee of the technical board unanimously voted to recommend a coöperative federal-state system, along lines similar to the Wagner-Lewis bill.[74] The executive committee of the technical board, on the other hand, continued to be divided. Messrs. Altmeyer, Riefler, and Viner favored the Wagner-Lewis plan; Dr. Lubin, a federal system. Finally, both committees agreed upon a report on "The Major Alternative Plans for the Administration of Unemployment Insurance," in which the respective advantages of the "federal," "Wagner-Lewis," and "subsidy" plans were discussed impartially, and the Committee on Economic Security was advised that it would be impossible to proceed much further with the work of the staff and the technical board until the committee had reached a definite decision as between these several alternatives.

This report was the main subject for consideration in the

74. In September, this committee unanimously favored a federal system; in November it was unanimous for a coöperative federal-state plan.

meeting of the Committee on Economic Security held on November 9, 1934. At this meeting there was a full attendance of the committee, and in addition there were present Messrs. Altmeyer, Eliot, Riefler, Viner, and Lubin of the executive committee of the technical board and Mr. Hansen, the chairman of its Committee on Unemployment Insurance, and also Dr. Stewart, the staff member heading the study of unemployment compensation. Statements in favor of a federal system were made by Dr. Lubin and Dr. Stewart; in favor of a federal-state coöperative plan, by Messrs. Riefler, Hansen, Viner, and Altmeyer. The subject was discussed at length among members of the committee and the other persons in attendance. At the conclusion of the discussion, a motion was offered by Mr. Hopkins and unanimously adopted by the members of the committee that all thought of an exclusively federal system be abandoned. The unanimous view of the committee also appeared to be that the Wagner-Lewis plan for federal-state coöperation was preferable to the subsidy plan, but this issue was not definitely disposed of.

This decision of the Committee on Economic Security, in favor of a coöperative federal-state system of unemployment insurance, was promptly transmitted to the President by Chairman Perkins. He expressed his agreement with this conclusion and stated that he was willing to include a definite announcement to this effect in his forthcoming address to the National Conference on Economic Security. This was done by the President in his address to the National Conference on Economic Security,[75] delivered at the White

75. At this National Conference, one round-table session was devoted to unemployment compensation. In this session the presiding officer was Dean Joseph H. Willetts of the Wharton School of Finance and Commerce, and the discussion leaders, H. W. Story of the Allis-Chalmers Manufacturing Company; Paul H. Douglas, of the University of Chicago; Thomas Kennedy, secretary of the United Mine Workers of America; and Miss Josephine Goldmark, of the National

118

House late in the afternoon of November 14. In this address, the President stated that the program which he would recommend to the incoming Congress would include unemployment insurance to be developed as "a cooperative federal-state undertaking," with the administration vested in the states, but with the federal government participating to encourage the states to enact unemployment insurance laws and holding and investing all unemployment reserve funds, to the end that these funds might serve "the purpose of decreasing rather than of increasing unemployment." The President, also, again expressed his concern that unemployment insurance must not be allowed to become a dole through the mingling of insurance and relief: "It is not charity. It must be financed by contributions, not taxes." He also again urged that unemployment insurance should be set up in such a way as to encourage the stabilization of employment.

Consumers' League. Like all other programs of the National Conference, this particular round-table was designed to give equal representation to advocates of the opposing views on the principal controversial points: in this case, unemployment insurance versus unemployment reserves. Professor Douglas and Mr. Kennedy were known to favor pooled unemployment insurance funds; Mr. Story and Miss Goldmark, unemployment reserves. These respective points of view were in fact presented by these discussion leaders, and this subject seemed to be the one uppermost throughout this round-table session. Mr. Kennedy, however, also injected the issue of a federal versus a state unemployment system, advocating an exclusively federal system. This subject was not directly touched upon by any of the other speakers, but Professor Douglas stated that since a federal system was apparently out of the question, legislation along the general lines of the Wagner-Lewis bill of the preceding Congress should be enacted. Subsequent to the National Conference, at which, apparently, he first became aware of the controversy over the Wagner-Lewis and the subsidy methods for a coöperative federal-state system, Professor Douglas wrote the committee that he desired to have his speech which he made at the conference corrected to strike out the endorsement of the Wagner-Lewis plan and substitute therefor an endorsement of the subsidy plan. This was done and the committee

119

This address of the President was reported in all of the newspapers as definitely committing the Administration to a program of unemployment insurance to be secured through joint federal-state action. The President, in his address specifically urged all persons in attendance at the conference and others interested in social security to make their plans on the basis that there must be both federal and state action before unemployment insurance could be established in this country. He called specific attention to the fact that the great majority of the legislatures would convene in January and urged that attention be given at once to the necessary state legislation, which rested entirely with the people back home.

While the great majority of those who heard the President's address, as well as the newspaper reports, got the

---

widely distributed the altered speech containing Douglas' endorsement of the subsidy plan.

At the close of this round-table session, Mrs. Irene S. Chubb of Webster Grove, Missouri, offered a motion that the National Conference on Economic Security go on record in endorsement of the Wagner-Lewis bill. This motion was accepted by the chairman, despite the fact that Secretary Perkins and President Graham (the general presiding officer of the National Conference) had in their opening statements stressed the fact that the conference was not expected to make any recommendations on legislation, but was intended merely to afford an opportunity for the presentation of all differing opinions on the major problems connected with economic security. This fact was pointed out in the discussion on Mrs. Chubb's motion and she finally withdrew this motion. Based on this incident, however, newspaper reports of the conference included statements that the conference had turned down a resolution in favor of the Wagner-Lewis bill. Opponents of the Wagner-Lewis plan of federal-state coöperation later, also, used this incident in support of a claim that the National Conference did not favor this plan, but preferred the subsidy plan. This was a complete misconstruction. The subsidy plan was not mentioned by anyone at any other meeting held on this day. Up to this time, discussion of the subsidy plan had been confined entirely to the members of the staff of the Committee on Economic Security and the technical board.

impression that the question of an exclusively federal versus a federal-state system of unemployment insurance had been definitely settled, this was not accepted as final by some members of the staff who strongly supported a federal system. Despite the President's statement, this issue was revived at a meeting of "experts" on unemployment insurance, which was held under the chairmanship of Dr. Stewart on November 15, the day following the National Conference on Economic Security. This was an invited gathering, with Dr. Stewart making the selection of the persons to be invited. Most of the discussion at this meeting concerned the type of federal legislation to be recommended. Of seventeen persons voting on the question, fourteen favored a national system and only three a coöperative federal-state plan. The majority of those favoring a federal system also voted in favor of the so-called subsidy plan, if federal-state coöperation was deemed necessary.

Unemployment Compensation
before the Advisory Council

As was the situation with the staff and the technical board, the advisory council was much more interested in unemployment compensation than in any other subject. This matter was brought before the council at the opening of its sessions, in the address of Secretary Perkins, who stated that the committee felt bound by the President's declarations of policy in his speech at the National Conference, but considered all other matters still open for decision. This subject was also the first one dealt with in my "Suggestions for a Long-Time and an Immediate Program for Economic Security," which I had prepared to serve as a basis for the beginning of the deliberations of the council. On the second day of its sessions, the advisory council was furnished by Dr. Stewart with a copy of the minutes of his meeting of experts

121

on unemployment insurance held on the preceding day, and at that time it also called before it Messrs. Stewart, Murray, and Williamson to give information on this subject, and later also Mrs. Armstrong. At no time, however, did the advisory council confer with the technical board, although this was suggested both by Secretary Perkins and myself. Instead, it relied principally upon the advice of Dr. Stewart, who attended all meetings except those of the first day, and also all meetings of the Unemployment Insurance Committee of the advisory council.

While the advisory council received the report of the "experts" in favor of federal administration of unemployment compensation, it disposed of this subject immediately thereafter, taking the position that a federal system could no longer be considered in view of the President's statements. It devoted much time, however, to the question whether the coöperative federal-state system should be developed along the lines of the Wagner-Lewis bill or of the subsidy plan. It also gave a great deal of attention to the standards to be written into the federal law, the contribution (tax) rates to be paid by employers, the advisability of employee and governmental contributions, individual employer and industry funds or accounts, the possibility of a federal reinsurance and interstate transfer fund, and the relation of the federal administrative agency to the Department of Labor.

As previously recited, no decisions on any of these controversial issues were reached until the meetings held December 6–8. The story of the action taken on the type of the federal law to be recommended and on sources of contributions and contribution rates has already been told in sufficient detail.[76] On the issue of pooled funds versus individual employer accounts, the council, without a record vote, decided to recommend that states be given a free hand

76. On pages 53–60 of this memorandum on the meetings of the advisory council.

to adopt either system, but subject to the condition that 1 per cent on their payrolls of the employers' contributions be required to be paid into a state pooled fund. The proposed interstate re-insurance and transfer fund was dropped as too difficult to work out on short notice, but a recommendation was made that the administrative board should study the question and try to work out provisions for such a fund, for adoption in later years by Congress. On the question of administration, the council adopted a compromise, under which most of the functions of the federal government in relation to unemployment compensation were to be performed by the Department of Labor, but the approval of state laws and the determination of major questions of policy were to be left to a quasi-independent board within the Department of Labor, composed of the Secretary of Labor, the Secretary of Commerce, and five appointees of the President.

Besides these major questions, the advisory council considered section by section a draft federal bill prepared by Dr. Stewart and Mr. Murray. There was considerable objection to this procedure on the part of several members, particularly Miss Abbott and Miss Dewson, and on at least one occasion the council voted not to recommend any bill, but to leave matters of detail to the Committee on Economic Security. Mr. Kellogg, however, was very insistent that the council should recommend a complete program, and his view ultimately prevailed. At the conclusion of its consideration of detailed provisions of the federal bill, however, it adopted a motion by Mr. Folsom, which was incorporated in the report of the advisory council and read as follows:

The majority of the Council are of the opinion that the minimum standards herein provided should be incorporated in the federal law, but the Council realizes that as a matter of policy, in order to secure federal and state legislation, the Committee on Economic Security may find it advisable to omit or amend some of these standards in the Federal act.

In similar vein, the council adopted a resolution qualifying its prior endorsement of the subsidy plan for federal-state coöperation by a vote of 9 to 7, with 6 members absent or not voting, to the effect that this vote was to be taken as merely indicating the preferences of the individual members of the council, that all recognized that both the Wagner-Lewis and subsidy plans had distinct merits and appreciated that the decision between these plans had to be made by the Committee on Economic Security.

Following these meetings at which the advisory council decided what recommendations it should make on unemployment compensation, it held another meeting (on December 15) in which it went over the draft of its report prepared by its drafting committee. At this meeting, the major question of employee contributions was reopened. In successive votes, the council refused, 8 to 10, to recommend employee contributions, and, 13 to 4, placed itself on record against a tax on employees as a part of the federal legislation.

Thereafter, as has been recited, the advisory council filed its completed report with the Committee on Economic Security, and four supplemental or minority statements were also presented by some of the members of the council. Later on these were presented to the congressional committees of both houses which conducted the hearings on the economic security bill, and they were published in full in the *Hearings*. No bill incorporating the recommendations of the advisory council, however, was ever drafted, and, as far as I know, no amendment based upon any of the recommendations was ever presented.

Report of the Committee on Economic Security

As recited, the Committee on Economic Security was deeply engaged in the final consideration of its recommendations before the advisory council made its report. Before

124

it completed its work it had received this report and also had before it recommendations on unemployment insurance made by the Committee on Industrial Relations of the Business Advisory and Planning Council of the Department of Commerce and by various private agencies. It also knew what Dr. Stewart who headed its staff studies on this subject would recommend, although it did not actually receive his report until after it had informally reported its recommendations to the President.[77] In reaching its decisions, however, the committee relied more upon interchange of views among the members and the advice of the technical board and their own departmental subordinates than upon anything else.

At the very outset of its final deliberations, the committee decided against federal dictation regarding the content of state unemployment compensation laws. It reached the conclusion that the federal bill should contain only a few necessary standards, leaving to the states complete freedom as to benefit rates, employee and governmental contributions, and practically everything else that is customarily included in an unemployment compensation law. Instead of recommending restrictions upon state legislation, it decided to include in its report suggestions for state legislation, with brief comments giving the reasons for the recommendations, and to follow this up by model state bills incorporating these recommendations to be sent to the governors of all states, but with the explanation that they represented suggestions only, which the states were free to follow or not to follow as they saw fit.[78]

77. Dr. Stewart's report favored an exclusively federal system of unemployment insurance, and, as a second choice, a coöperative federal-state system of the subsidy type. The Logan bill (S. 214, 74th Congress, First Session) incorporated this latter proposal but never received any real consideration in Congress.

78. Two drafts of state unemployment compensation laws—one for a pooled fund and the other for an individual employer account system—both with various alternative sections, were sent to all

Later the committee again considered whether it should recommend federal legislation of the Wagner-Lewis or subsidy types. It again devoted several hours to the discussion of this problem and once more decided in favor of the Wagner-Lewis bill. At my suggestion, even this decision was at that time treated as tentative, pending the completion of studies then under way to determine whether there was any state in which it was clearly impossible to deposit the unemployment compensation funds in the federal treasury (which would have rendered undesirable the Wagner-Lewis type of federal legislation). These studies were made independently by Mr. Eliot and Dr. Harris, both of whom reached the conclusion that there was no state in which the constitution clearly forbade the deposit of unemployment compensation funds in the United States Treasury. Accordingly, the question was not again brought before the committee, and its report favored the tax-offset proposal of the Wagner-Lewis bill in preference to the tax remission contemplated in the subsidy plan.

On other questions of policy, there was even less division among the members of the committee. Secretary Perkins regarded the low contribution rates in the first two years as unfortunate, but Secretary Morgenthau was very insistent that rates should be geared to business recovery and should not alarm businessmen. He was supported in this view by

governors and to all interim legislative committees concerned with unemployment insurance early in February. These were accompanied by an explanatory memorandum and a summary of actuarial data on unemployment by states, to serve as a basis for the determination of contribution and benefit rates. None of this material was ever submitted to the members of the committee, but was sent out on my own responsibility, in accordance with a promise to this effect made in the committee's report. These model bills included all features required to be inserted in the state act by the original economic security bill as well as all suggestions made by the committee for state legislation.

Secretary Wallace and finally carried the entire committee with him. Secretary Morgenthau was, also, greatly in favor of employee contributions. For a long time, he insisted that if the report of the committee did not include a recommendation for employee contributions, he would have to make a minority report. He never changed his views, but in the end yielded to a personal appeal of Secretary Perkins that the committee ought to present a unanimous front, and signed the report without appending thereto a statement of his own views on this subject.

The question of pooled funds versus individual employer accounts was very thoroughly considered by the committee, but all members were in agreement that the states should be left free to adopt the type of unemployment compensation law they preferred. Mr. Hopkins and Secretary Perkins did not like individual employer accounts and Miss Josephine Roche of the Treasury Department and Messrs. Tugwell and Frank of the Department of Agriculture (all of whom had important roles in the Committee's action at this stage) still less so. On the other hand, it was known to all members of the committee that the President was anxious that the federal law should give encouragement to employers to stabilize their business and for this reason was inclined toward the Wisconsin type of unemployment compensation law. The provisions on this point included in the committee's report were not finally settled until the long informal evening session which was held at the home of Secretary Perkins just before Christmas. The restriction upon individual employer accounts included in the committee's recommendations— that states permitting individual employer accounts must require employers to contribute at least 1 per cent on their payrolls to the central pooled fund—was first advocated by Dr. Altmeyer and was accepted by the committee as a reasonable compromise. The very drastic restrictions on guaranteed employment accounts were suggested by Miss Roche and were accepted by the committee in the thought that they would operate to make guaranteed employment accounts practically impossible.

The President's Message of January 17, 1935

Complete agreement relating to unemployment insurance (as well as upon all other recommendations to be included in the report) was, as recited above, arrived at before Christmas and communicated to the President on December 24. These recommendations were not officially made public, however, until the President transmitted the report of the committee to Congress in his special message of January 17, 1935. In this message, the President said, on this subject:

With respect to unemployment compensation, I have concluded that the most practical proposal is the levy of a uniform federal payroll tax, 90 per cent of which should be allowed as an offset to employers contributing under a compulsory State unemployment compensation act. The purpose of this is to afford a requirement of a reasonably uniform character for all States cooperating with the Federal Government and to promote and encourage the passage of unemployment compensation laws in the States. The 10 per cent not thus offset should be used to cover the costs of Federal and State administration of this broad system. Thus, States will largely administer unemployment compensation, assisted and guided by the Federal Government. An unemployment compensation system should be constructed in such a way as to afford every practicable aid and incentive toward the larger purpose of employment stabilization. This can be helped by the intelligent planning of both public and private employment. It also can be helped by correlating the system with public employment so that a person who has exhausted his benefits may be eligible for some form of public work as is recommended in this report. Moreover, in order to encourage the stabilization of private employment, Federal legislation should not foreclose the States from establishing means for inducing industries to afford an even greater stabilization of employment.

The first draft of this message of the President was prepared by Dr. Altmeyer. This did not include the sentences given above relating to the stabilization of employment, nor anything else along this line. It is my belief that this language was added by Professor Moley, who was asked by the President to come to Washington to assist him with this message. Professor Moley, like the President, did not like the restrictions upon this type of law which were included in the committee's report, as the President stated quite clearly in the message.

Original Bill

The original economic security bill, which was introduced immediately after the President's message, followed exactly the recommendations of the Committee on Economic Security. As has been recited, this bill was largely drafted by Mr. Eliot, the counsel of the committee. Mr. Eliot personally believed that the standards with which state laws must comply, which were included in Section 602 of the original bill (Section 903 [a] of the final act), should be made conditions merely for grants for the administration of unemployment insurance, instead of conditions for the recognition of state laws for tax-offset purposes. I also consistently advocated that no standards should be included in the federal act to which the state laws must comply except that all moneys collected under the state laws must be used for unemployment compensation purposes. Because the committee had reached contrary decisions, we included the standards which the committee had decided should go into the federal law as conditions for the tax offset in the original economic security bill.

Unemployment Compensation
in the Congressional Hearings

In the hearings on the economic security bill, the members of the congressional committees manifested relatively little interest in unemployment insurance, being largely engrossed in old age pensions. All witnesses who had anything to do with the development of the program on economic security, however, devoted a large part of their testimony to this subject. As already related, advocates of the subsidy plan made every effort to get the Congress to reverse the decision of the Committee on Economic Security in favor of the tax-offset plan and Mr. Epstein presented a complete substitute for the unemployment insurance titles of the bill. Mr. Kellogg and Mr. Green and a few others urged higher contribution rates; Messrs. Folsom, Story, and Harriman, the elimination of restrictions upon individual employer accounts and greater encouragement of the regularization of employment. Finally, there were ultraconservatives opposed to unemployment compensation in any form and radicals who advocated the Lundeen bill. While all of these views were earnestly presented, it is my belief that they influenced the ultimate content of the Social Security Act but slightly, with the exception of Mr. Folsom's arguments for greater freedom to the states in the matter of encouraging the regularization of employment, which greatly impressed the Senate Finance Committee.

Revision by the House Ways and Means Committee

In the executive sessions of the House Ways and Means Committee and the Senate Finance Committee, in which the economic security bill was gone over section by section, no mention was made of the subsidy plan. The congressional draftsmen considered this plan to be unconstitutional, while

130

they regarded the tax-offset plan as probably constitutional. In all my conversations with members of Congress, no one ever mentioned the subsidy plan except Senator Wagner, who prior to the introduction of the economic security bill expressed his opposition to this plan.

The matters affecting unemployment insurance which were considered by the congressional committees were detailed provisions of the original bill affecting unemployment compensation which were made by the Ways and Means Committee and the reasons therefor, as I understand them, were the following:

Coverage of Federal Tax. The original bill, following the recommendations of the Committee on Economic Security, applied to all employers in the United States who, during the taxable year, employed four or more persons in each of at least thirteen weeks. Exempted from the tax were only the federal government and the state governments and their political subdivisions, and it was specifically provided that, where a subcontractor or contractor was not subject to the tax, his employees should be considered as employees of the principal contractor or employer. The Ways and Means Committee amended this coverage to exclude, in addition to the federal, state, and local governments, agricultural labor, domestic service in a private home, employment as a member of the crew of a vessel on any of the navigable waters of the United States, employment by an immediate member of the family, and employment by an organization operated exclusively for religious, charitable, scientific, literary, or educational purposes and without private profit. This last exclusion was similar in effect to the exclusion which was made from the tax levied for old age insurance purposes, but was justified on a different ground. Mr. Beaman told the congressional committees that the states could not tax vessels because the federal government has exclusive jurisdiction of all matters of admiralty, and the committees felt that, under the circumstances, it would be unfair to subject them to the federal tax. The other exclusions were not advocated specifically by anyone, but were suggested by members of the committee. Agricultural labor and domestic services were excluded as a matter of course. The exclusion of the crews of vessels on the navigable waters of the United States was suggested by Mr. Beaman, the chief draftsman of the House, on the ground that it would be difficult to collect the federal tax if vessels were included.

The provision of the original bill applying the federal tax to employers of four or more during thirteen weeks of the taxable year was changed by the Ways and Means Committee to ten or more in twenty weeks of the taxable year. This change provoked considerable discussion and was made largely at the instance of Congressman Fuller, who wanted the canneries in his district to be exempted. An important factor in this connection was the fact that the Wagner-Lewis bill of the preceding Congress applied to employers of ten or more during twenty weeks of the year. Congressman Cooper, one of the most influential majority members of the Ways and Means Committee, was the chairman of the subcommittee which conducted hearings on the Wagner-Lewis bill and it was he who suggested that the pending bill should be changed to provide the same coverage as the measure of the preceding Congress.

Rate of Tax. The original bill, like the measure reported by the Ways and Means Committee, contemplated a maximum rate of 3 per cent on the employers' payrolls in 1938 and thereafter, and likewise provided for lower rates in 1936 and 1937. It geared these rates for the first two years, however, to business recovery, providing that for the year 1936 the rate should be 1 per cent, if the adjusted index of total industrial production of the Federal Reserve Board for the

132

twelve months ending September 30, 1935, was not more than 84 per cent of the average for the years 1923–1925, and that it should be 2 per cent if it was more than 84 per cent but less than 95 per cent of such average, and 3 per cent if 95 per cent or above; similarly, it provided that the rate for 1937 should be determined on the same basis, using the twelve months ending September 30, 1936, as the standard. This provision was objected to by the representatives of the Treasury who attended the executive sessions of the Ways and Means Committee, primarily because it appeared in March, 1935, that the average of the monthly production indices of the Federal Reserve Board for the twelve months ending September 30, 1935, would be just around 84 per cent. Throughout, the attitude of the Treasury was that as light a burden as possible should be put on industry at the outset and the Treasury feared that the formula of the original bill would result in a 2 per cent rate in the first year. This was greatly desired by the Department of Labor, but not by the Treasury. The committee adopted the view of the Treasury; in part, perhaps, because it was stated that the Federal Reserve Board contemplated a revision of its index of industrial production, but mainly because most members of the committee agreed with the view that industry should have assurance that the rate in the first year would not exceed 1 per cent and in the second year would not exceed 2 per cent. The bill reported by the Ways and Means Committee, consequently, definitely fixed the rate of the federal tax at 1 per cent for the year 1936, 2 per cent for 1937, and 3 per cent for 1938 and thereafter.

Tax Offset and Additional Credit for Stabilization. The Ways and Means Committee accepted without question the general plan recommended by the Committee on Economic Security for an offset against the federal tax of payments made under state unemployment compensation laws, up to

90 per cent of the federal tax. Congressmen Cooper, Vinson, and Hill, the three most active members of the committee, however, questioned the constitutionality of the provisions suggested by the Committee on Economic Security, that an additional credit should be allowed to employers in excess of the amount which they paid under state unemployment compensation laws, if the state law permitted them to reduce their contribution rates, because they had built up adequate reserves or had an unusually favorable experience with regard to the amount of unemployment within their plants. The three congressmen mentioned took the position that this additional credit provision destroyed the uniformity of the tax and would operate to make it unconstitutional. It was pointed out to the committee that the President was greatly interested in setting up unemployment compensation on such a basis that employers would have an incentive to reduce unemployment and that the additional credit provision was the only one in the entire bill which afforded such an incentive. After a prolonged discussion, and at the close of a day, a motion by Congressman Cooper was adopted to strike out this provision. This motion was carried by a majority of two, with nearly half the members of the committee absent.[79]

79. Despite the narrow margin by which this motion was adopted, in the absence of so many members, no motion was ever made for reconsideration of this action, although such a motion, if offered, might have carried. The reason that no motion for reconsideration was made was an incident which developed on the next day following the action of the committee. At the opening of the session of the next meeting of the committee, Congressman Treadway, the ranking Republican member of the committee, read a telegram which he received from Roger S. Hoar of South Milwaukee, Wisconsin, a personal acquaintance, in which Hoar stated that the committee had voted to eliminate the additional credit provision and that he understood that Treadway had been absent and asked that he make a motion for reconsideration. Treadway indignantly protested that this telegram indicated that some violation of the executive character of the committee's sessions had occurred, inas-

Mr. Beaman, the chief draftsman of the House, interpreted the Cooper motion to include not only the elimination of the additional credit section, but also of the provision allowing states to have either a pooled-fund or an individual employer account type of unemployment compensation law. I did not believe that this was the intention of the committee, but felt that I could not bring up the matter, because the Wisconsin law was involved. In conference, the House conferees readily assented to the Senate amendment restoring the provisions of the original bill in this respect and stated that they had not intended to bar free choice by the states as to the type of law they wished to enact.

Standards in State Laws. No change of any importance was made by the Ways and Means Committee in the conditions set forth in the law for the approval of state unemployment compensation acts for tax-offset purposes. In fact, the only change made throughout the course of the consideration of the social security legislation in Congress was in the first condition. This read in the original bill that compensation must be paid through public employment offices. This was amended in the Senate by adding the qualifying, "to the extent that such offices exist and are designated by the state for the purpose." As revised by the conference committee and as included in the final act, the provision became that

---

much as this outsider apparently had information regarding the vote taken on the previous day. In the course of this meeting, the source of this leak was revealed as a communication by Mr. Eliot to Dr. Altmeyer, which in turn was transmitted to Paul Raushenbush, the director of the Unemployment Compensation Division of the Industrial Commission of Wisconsin, who communicated with Hoar. Treadway himself favored the additional credit provision, but was opposed to the entire bill and anxious to "gum up the works." The incident recited operated to discredit the influence of the representatives of the Committee on Economic Security and was directly responsible for the fact that the Ways and Means Committee struck out the additional credit provision, although it is doubtful whether a majority of the members of the committee really favored this action.

compensation shall be paid through public employment offices "or such other agencies as the board may approve."[80]

80. The other five conditions remained as in the original bill. The second condition, that no compensation shall be paid until two years after contributions begin, was recommended by the Committee on Economic Security because it was expected that the states would fix their benefits rates on the basis of 3 per cent contributions, but would collect only 1 per cent in the first year and 2 per cent in the second year, so that this condition really amounted to requiring the collection of one year's contributions before benefits could be paid. A reserve of one year's contributions was deemed absolutely essential to prevent exhaustion of the unemployment reserve funds at the very outset. The third condition relating to the deposit of state unemployment reserve funds in the United States Treasury is discussed under the heading "Unemployment Trust Fund," on page 136 of this book and in Note 81 below. The fourth condition—that all moneys withdrawn from the Unemployment Trust Fund must be used for the payment of compensation—was considered by the committee the most important of all. In the congressional hearings, Industrial Commissioner Andrews of New York suggested an amendment of this paragraph to permit some of the unemployment reserve funds to be used for administrative purposes. This suggestion was not accepted by the Committee on Economic Security or the congressional committees because it was felt that the federal aid for administration would prove sufficient to cover at least most of the administrative costs, and that, if any state required more, the additional amount should be raised by general taxation, instead of being taken out of the unemployment reserve funds, reducing the amount available for the payment of benefits.

The fifth condition, relating to labor standards, was copied verbatim from the Wagner-Lewis bill of the preceding session. In the meetings of the advisory council, the employer members objected to the clause relating to company unions and the council recommended that this clause be changed to make the condition applicable to labor unions as well as to company unions. This was done over the objection of Mr. Green, and the Committee on Economic Security felt that his position was well taken. The congressional committees accepted the condition without question.

The sixth condition was one which was inserted in the bill at the insistence of Jerome Frank, then of the legal division of the A.A.A. It was Frank's theory that unless a clause of this kind were included in the bill, the courts might hold that employers acquired a vested right under state laws establishing an unemployment reserve type of

Unemployment Trust Fund. No changes of much importance were made by the congressional committees in the sections relating to the unemployment trust fund and the deposit in this fund of all moneys collected by the states for unemployment compensation purposes. These sections were inserted in the bill to carry out an oft-expressed idea of the President and were not seriously questioned by anyone.[81]

---

compensation system against subsequent abandonment of this type of law. No one connected with the Committee on Economic Security thought there was anything to the point, but the language was inserted in the bill to appease Mr. Frank and to get the signature of Secretary Wallace to the committee's report. The construction subsequently given to this condition by the Social Security Board, that it barred a return to employers going out of business of funds left over in their individual employer accounts, was never suggested by anyone at any stage of the development and consideration of the Social Security Act.

81. The views of the President on this subject were clearly expressed in the special message of June 8, 1934, in his address to the National Conference on Economic Security, and in his special message of January 17, 1935. These views were most strongly approved by the Business Advisory and Planning Council of the Department of Commerce and by all businessmen consulted in connection with the development of the social security program. Similarly, they were approved by all witnesses who discussed these provisions in the congressional hearings except Mr. Epstein. The handling and management of large reserve funds was made the subject of a special staff study by Messrs. Powell and Swayzee, under the guidance of a special committee of the technical board composed of Messrs. Hansen, Riefler, and Viner.

As worked out by these members of the staff and the technical board, the plan differed from that finally adopted in that it provided for the deposit of the state unemployment reserve funds in the federal reserve banks and gave control of the investment and liquidation of these funds to the Federal Reserve Board, instead of the United States Treasury. This plan was endorsed by the advisory council, without dissent by anyone. In the final consideration of its recommendations, however, the Committee on Economic Security substituted the Treasury for the federal reserve banks and the Secretary of the Treasury for the Federal Reserve Board. This was insisted upon by the Secretary of the Treasury, although his representative on the technical board, Dr. Viner, felt very strongly that the control of the

Federal Administration. At all stages of the consideration of the social security legislation, the representatives of the Department of Labor on the Committee on Economic Security urged very strongly that the administration of unemployment compensation (insofar as it was to be a federal function) belonged in this department. This was not liked by many employers, who felt that the Department of Labor was too closely identified with organized labor. Dr. Stewart of the staff of the committee favored an independent governmental corporation to administer unemployment insurance, under the mistaken assumption that such a corporation would not have to go to Congress for changes in contribution rates, benefits, etc. After quite extensive discussion of the problem, the advisory council, as already mentioned, recommended a compromise under which the administration was nominally vested in the Department of Labor, but the real control was given to a quasi-independent board, of which the Secretary of Labor was only one of seven members.

---

reserve funds should be vested in the Federal Reserve Board. This was considered as a theoretically sound position by the Secretary of the Treasury and his other advisors, but only if the Treasury really controlled the Federal Reserve Board. It was expected that, in the banking legislation which would come before Congress, the Federal Reserve Board would be reorganized and brought under the closer control of the national administration. As it was not certain, however, that such legislation would be passed, the Secretary of the Treasury insisted that the control of the reserve funds must be in his hands. This was agreed to by all other people connected with the committee, with the understanding that, if Congress passed legislation bringing the Federal Reserve Board under the control of the national administration, the provisions in the Social Security Act relating to the unemployment trust fund could be modified to substitute the Federal Reserve Board for the Secretary of the Treasury. Actually, the banking bill dragged on in Congress about as long as the social security bill, and no proposal to substitute the Federal Reserve Board for the Secretary of the Treasury was ever made at any stage of the consideration of the social security bill in Congress.

138

Mr. Hopkins of the Committee on Economic Security at various times expressed himself privately in favor of the creation of a federal department of public welfare, to administer unemployment compensation and all of the various forms of public assistance. In the meetings of the committee, however, he and all of the other members of the committee agreed that the administration of unemployment compensation should be vested in the Department of Labor. In the report of the committee and in the original bill, a Social Security Board was created to be composed of appointees of the President, but this board was placed within the Department of Labor, with control of all personnel vested in the Secretary of Labor.

There was little discussion of this matter in the hearings in either house, but it became one of the major questions in the consideration of the bill in the executive sessions of the congressional committees.[82] This question was passed over in all of the early executive sessions of the Ways and Means Committee. It was not taken up until several of the more important members of the committee (Chairman Doughton and Messrs. Hill, Cooper, and Vinson) had conferred with the President regarding the points in the original bill upon which he would insist. In this conference, as I was subse-

82. There was great antipathy among the members of the Ways and Means Committee toward the Department of Labor. The major source of difficulty was the resentment of members of Congress over the insistence of the Department of Labor that the persons employed in the offices of the United States Employment Service must be selected on a merit basis. There were many stories current among the congressmen of curt treatment to which they claimed they had been subjected when talking about appointments in the Employment Service to Mr. Persons, the director of the service, and to Secretary Perkins herself. A further factor entered into the situation that some of the members of the Ways and Means Committee identified the Department of Labor with organized labor and wanted to take a slap at organized labor for its attitude towards the Administration's work relief bill.

quently informed by the congressional members, the President stated that he wanted the Social Security Board to be within the Department of Labor, but he also indicated that he did not intend to dictate to Congress. The net result was that these members got the impression that the President would not object strongly if the Social Security Board were made an independent agency. The matter was then brought to a vote and a motion to this effect carried almost unanimously.

Changes in the Senate

As has been recited, no changes whatsoever were made in the social security bill on the floor of the House. Several amendments affecting unemployment compensation were offered, but like all other amendments (except the Townsend plan) received very little consideration.

As has also been related,[83] the House bill was in many respects not satisfactory to the Committee on Economic Security and it went to work promptly to get it changed in the Senate. In relation to unemployment compensation, the major amendments which it suggested were to restore to the states freedom of choice with regard to the type of unemployment compensation law they would have to adopt to entitle their employes to the tax offset and to put the Social Security Board back into the Department of Labor;[84] and on both of these amendments the committee had the complete support of the President. These amendments were presented to the Senate Finance Committee by Secretary Perkins in her appearance before this committee in executive session, and both were adopted but not exactly as desired by the secretary. Plus these, several other amendments to

83. See Part I, page 91 ff. of this book.
84. Dr. Altmeyer and Secretary Perkins urged increase of the initial federal tax rates to 2 per cent or restoration of the provisions of the original bill on this point, but received no encouragement from anyone.

140

this part of the bill were recommended by the Senate committee, all of them without much disagreement.

The major changes made by the Senate committee and subsequently concurred in by the Senate were the following:

Coverage. The Senate committee restored the provision of the original bill making the federal tax applicable to all employers of four or more employees in thirteen weeks of the taxable year. The committee extended somewhat the exemptions of charitable, religious, and educational institutions, to include hospitals and childrens' home-finding societies. It struck out the exemption of the crews of vessels on the navigable waters of the United States, doing so, on the recommendation of the chairman, to have something to trade with in conference.

Type of State Law and Additional Credit Provisions. The Senate committee, unanimously and without much discussion, restored the provisions of the original bill permitting the states to determine for themselves whether they wished to have pooled funds or individual employer accounts or a combination of these systems.[85] It also restored the provisions relating to additional credits to employers permitted lower contribution rates by state laws because they had stabilized their employment. In doing so, it put much less drastic limitations upon additional credits than were included in the original bill, striking out entirely the restriction that states permitting individual employer accounts must require contributions by the employers of at least 1 per cent on their payrolls to a central pooled fund.

The adoption of this amendment reflected not only the distinct preference of many members of the Senate com-

85. These changes were known as the La Follette amendment, which was introduced by Senator La Follette. The amendment was drafted by Mr. Eliot, acting under instructions from Senator La Follette. His instructions were based upon suggestions made by Paul Raushenbush, director of the Unemployment Compensation Division of the Industrial Commission of Wisconsin.

mittee for the Wisconsin type of unemployment compensation law, but was strongly influenced by the decision of the United States Supreme Court in the Railroad Retirement Act case. This decision cast doubt upon the constitutionality of pooled funds. After this decision, there was little question that if Congress passed any law relating to unemployment compensation, it would permit the states to modify their rates in accordance with the risk and experience of the employers, since it appeared doubtful whether it would be constitutional for them not to do so.

Federal Administrative Agency. The Senate put the Social Security Board back in the Department of Labor, but with a provision which deprived the Secretary of Labor of control over the personnel of the board. It is my belief that this action of the Senate was taken because the President suggested to the chairman and perhaps other members of the Senate Finance Committee that he wanted the Social Security Board to be within the Department of Labor. But it was my feeling and also that of Mr. Eliot that the Senate committee was quite willing to yield to the House upon this point.

In the discussion of the social security act on the floor of the Senate, the unemployment compensation provisions received little attention. No amendments were offered affecting this part of the act other than those presented by the committee. The committee amendments were adopted without a roll call or division, and without any objections.

Conference Committee Changes

Unemployment compensation did not create much difficulty in the conference committee stages. The House conferees readily agreed to the Senate amendment permitting free choice to the states regarding the type of unemployment compensation act. Representative Hill, the most active member of the House conferees, objected to the additional credit provision of the La Follette amendment on the score that it would increase the chances that this part of the act would be held unconstitutional and the further count that it destroyed the main argument for federal action in relation to unemployment compensation, namely, uniformity of burdens upon employers throughout the country. He did not insist very long upon this point, however, and the House conferees accepted the La Follette amendment practically without change. In turn, the Senate conferees abandoned their amendment to place the Social Security Board within the Department of Labor, making only a perfunctory effort to maintain their position. The differences as to coverage were compromised by making the federal tax applicable to employers of eight or more employees. All matters relating to unemployment compensation were adjusted in the first two meetings of the conference committee. The long struggle which ensued related entirely to the Clark and Russell amendments to the old age security provisions of the bill.

OLD AGE ASSISTANCE

In the congressional hearings and in the executive sessions of the Committee on Ways and Means, as well as in the House debate, the major interest was in old age assistance. Very important changes were made in this part of the bill, principally by the House committee.

Title I of the original bill was very bitterly attacked, particularly by Senator Byrd, on the score that it vested in a federal department the power to dictate to the states to whom pensions should be paid and how much. In this position, Senator Byrd was supported by nearly all of the southern members of both committees, it being very evident that at least some southern senators feared that this measure might serve as an entering wedge for federal interference with the handling of the Negro question in the South. The southern members did not want to give authority to anyone in Washington to deny aid to any state because it discriminated against Negroes in the administration of old age assistance.

It was my position in the prolonged questioning which I underwent from Senator Byrd that there was no intention of federal dictation. The fact is that it had never occurred to any person connected with the Committee on Economic Security that the Negro question would come up in this connection. After the first days of the committee hearings, however, it was apparent that the bill could not be passed as it stood and that it would be necessary to tone down all clauses relating to supervisory control by the federal government.

The principal changes which were made by the Ways and Means Committee to this end were the following:

1. The conditions for the approval of state plans for old age assistance were stated negatively, with the effect that states might impose other conditions for old age assistance than those dealt with in the bill. Under the original bill, states could not impose any income or property restrictions, nor bar from old age assistance persons with criminal records or any other group of persons. Under the House bill, states were free to impose any conditions they saw fit, with the limitation that if they prescribed conditions as to age, residence, citizenship, etc., their restrictions might not be more stringent than those stipulated in the bill.

2. The House bill eliminated the provision that states must furnish assistance sufficient to provide, "when added to the income of the aged recipient, a reasonable subsistence compatible with decency and health." This provision was copied from the Massachusetts and New York laws and was very objectionable to southern members of Congress. The elimination of this provision left the states free to pay pensions of

144

any amount, however small, and yet recover 50 per cent of their costs from the federal government.

3. The provision that the methods of administration in the states must be satisfactory to the federal department was toned down by adding the qualification, "other than those relating to selection, tenure of office and compensation of personnel." This limitation was inserted because it was feared that the federal administrative agency would require the states to select their personnel on a merit basis, as had been done by the United States Employment Service. The members of Congress did not want any dictation by the federal government in this respect and inserted this limitation for the express purpose of allowing the states to appoint whomever they wished to administer old age assistance.

4. The provisions relating to the withdrawal of approval of state plans were somewhat toned down by inserting provisions to the effect that withdrawal of approval may occur only after notice to the state authorities, a fair hearing, and a finding that "in a substantial number of cases" the requirements of the federal act were being violated.

Plus these changes relating to the degree of federal control over the state administration of old age assistance, the original bill was modified to place the federal administration under the Social Security Board, instead of the Federal Emergency Relief Administrator. The action of the Committee on Economic Security in recommending administration of old age assistance by the Federal Emergency Relief Administrator was based upon the fact that he was responsible for the administration of relief. From the outset, the members of the Ways and Means Committee objected that this meant vesting the administration of old age assistance in an emergency agency, which, it was hoped, might soon be abolished; also that it placed old age assistance on a relief basis, which the committee was very anxious to avoid.

OLD AGE INSURANCE

Fundamental Change Made by the Congress

The Committee on Economic Security always considered and discussed the subject of old age security as falling into two parts:

1. Old age assistance to old people in need and on a needs basis, payable from general tax revenues.

2. Old age insurance, in the form of retirement annuities payable as a matter of right to wage-earners on retirement at a specified age, from funds to which they had themselves contributed.

This sort of a concept runs through all of the reports made by members of the staff on the subject, the report of the advisory council, the report of the Committee on Economic Security, and the President's message. It was understood that the validity of a federal old age insurance system was doubtful, but it was thought that it might be possible to set up such a system under the taxing power of Congress.

The original bill attempted to carry out this concept in as constitutionally plausible a form as possible; but there were no models to follow, the work had to be hastily done, and it was not at all satisfactory to Mr. Eliot. What he did was to separate the provisions relating to benefits from the provisions relating to the tax for old age insurance purposes, placing them in separted titles of the bill. The connection between the two, however, appeared in many provisions.

The entire plan was very objectionable to Mr. Beaman and seemed unconstitutional to the leading members of the Ways and Means Committee. These members agreed that if the benefits and the tax were really separated, the plan might be constitutional, but that there was no real separation between these two in the original bill. Beaman was then instructed to redraft the bill to make such a separation. The major change made was to drop all reference to an old age insurance fund. Instead of such a fund, an old age reserve account was set up in the Treasury; but the proceeds of the tax were not allocated to the old age reserve account or the payment of old age benefits. All provisions which related the benefits to the tax paid by the employers and their employees were eliminated, as well as all references to any contractual right to benefits. What the Ways and Means Committee and Beaman, acting under its instructions, sought to do was to get away from an insurance plan altogether, but to establish the equivalent of such a plan without resorting to a definite insurance scheme.

Other Changes Made by the Ways and Means Committee

Besides this major change in the form and general effect of the two titles of the bill dealing with this subject, many other important changes were made by the Ways and Means Committee from the plan suggested by the Committee on Economic Security incorporated in the original bill.

Tax Rates. The original bill (following the recommendations of the staff on old age security of the Committee on Economic Security) contemplated low tax rates over a long period of time for old age insurance purposes. These rates began with 0.5 per cent on employers and the same rate on employees for the five years 1937 to 1941 inclusive, with an increase to 1 per cent for the next five years (1942 to 1946, inclusive), and a similar increase of 0.5 per cent every five years therafter, until a maximum of 2.5 per cent on employers and 2.5 per cent on employees was reached in the year 1957 and thereafter. The benefits provided in this bill were such as the actuaries figured could be paid for by 5 per cent contributions on payroll over a lifetime of employment in industry. This meant that the combined rates on employers and employees would be adequate to pay the costs of the benefits only for employees entering the old age in-

147

surance system in 1957 and thereafter. In the first twenty years of the system far less would be collected than necessary to meet the costs computed on an actuarial basis. Due to the fact, however, that in any old age insurance system there are relatively few retirements during the early years, the amount collected in these first twenty years would nevertheless have been considerably greater than the disbursements during these years, so that the inadequacy of the rates would not create a serious financial problem until some years later. If the ultimate rate equaled only the actual current cost, however, the actuaries estimated that by 1965 a deficit would develop in the old age insurance fund, which would continue to increase until 1980. By that time this deficit would amount to approximately $1,400,000,000 per year. This deficit, the old age security staff proposed, should be met through contributions from the United States Treasury, although there was no way in which it could be guaranteed that when the deficits developed contributions would be actually made from general tax revenues, rather than be met through reduction of benefits or increase in the contribution rates.

The Committee on Economic Security was told by its staff that the taxes currently collected would not meet the costs of benefits after 1965 and it accepted the idea that the deficits resulting thereafter should be met from general tax sources. In all discussions preceding the committee's final decision on the recommendations it should make on old age security, the plan recommended by the staff was discussed in terms of larger benefits to workers approaching old age than could be paid for through their contributions and those of their employers, with the United States Government ultimately making up the resulting deficits from general tax sources. It is my belief that no member of the committee understood that payments in excess of contributions would be made not only to workers already approaching old age,

148

but to substantially all workers who entered employment prior to 1957. When Secretary Perkins and Mr. Hopkins, acting for the committee, presented its recommendations orally to the President on December 24, they described the recommendations on old age insurance in the terms used by the staff, and the President got the impression that the plan proposed contemplated payments in excess of contributions only to people approaching old age who did not have time to build up their own old age protection on a really adequate basis. He also accepted the argument made by the staff and the committee that the compulsory old age insurance system would reduce the costs of the noncontributory old age assistance grants and apparently formed the idea that the two programs combined would result in decreasing governmental costs as the years went on.

As previously recited, when the President examined in detail the tables included in the report of the Committee on Economic Security, immediately prior to his special message of January 17, he discovered that the tables on the committee's report did not jibe with his understanding of the old age security program. He noted that large deficits would result in 1965 and thereafter, to be met from general taxes; also that the benefit payments would exceed the combined contributions of employers and employees not only for all workers past middle age but for all younger workers and for all future workers entering employment prior to 1957. As has been recited, the President then insisted that the plan must be revised to make it entirely self-supporting.

To satisfy the President, the committee's report was altered at the last minute, avoiding a definite commitment to the tax and benefit rates recommended by the staff. The working out of new rates to make the plan self-supporting, however, required time. So the rates recommended by the staff had to be included in the original bill. The Committee on Economic Security, however, had definitely told the

President that it would revise these rates to accord with his views and would suggest an amendment to the Ways and Means Committee which would make the old age insurance system self-supporting (assuming the correctness of the actuarial calculations and continuance of the plan without material amendments in future years).

Actuarial calculations for this amendment were made by Mr. Latimer and Mr. Richter, representing the Committee on Economic Security, and Messrs. Reagh and Brown, actuaries in the employ of the Treasury Department. Several conferences were held on the matter in which the principal participants, besides the actuaries mentioned, were Dr. Altmeyer, Mr. Eliot, and myself of the Committee on Economic Security, and Messrs. Wilcox and Haas of the Treasury Department. When an agreement was finally reached, in accord with the President's views, it was presented to him by Secretaries Perkins and Morgenthau, Dr. Altmeyer, Mr. Haas, and myself. The President, after examining actuarial estimates based on the new proposals, expressed himself as satisfied, and it was then agreed that the new tax and benefit rates should be presented to the Ways and Means Committee by Secretary Morgenthau, representing the entire Committee on Economic Security.

Because Secretary Morgenthau presented this amendment, this proposal was termed the "Morgenthau amendment," and in all newspaper accounts was represented as if it was a proposal of the Secretary of the Treasury acting alone, whereas in fact it was an amendment recommended by the Committee on Economic Security and agreed to by all of its members. This amendment revised the bill to make the initial tax rate (for the years 1937, 1938 and 1939) 1 per cent on employers and 1 per cent on employees, and provided for increases of 0.5 per cent every three years, until a maximum of 3 per cent on employers and 3 per cent on employees would be reached in the year 1949, after which this rate was to be continued indefinitely. The actuaries estimated that the increased tax revenues yielded under this plan would enable the old age insurance system to remain entirely self-supporting, at least until 1980. At the same time, it would result in an ultimate reserve of nearly $50,000,000,000 as against a reserve of $14,000,000,000 estimated by the actuaries under the original plan. This large reserve was regarded by the President as creating a far less serious problem than the deficits after 1965 contemplated under the original plan.

The Morgenthau amendment was criticized before the Ways and Means Committee on the score of the large reserve which it would create by Messrs. Latimer and J. Douglas Brown, connected with the Committee on Economic Security, and before the Senate committee also by Mr. Folsom of the advisory council. Apparently, however, their arguments made little impression upon any members of either committee. The large reserve was used as argument against the bill by Senator Hastings on the floor of the Senate, but neither he nor any other member of either congressional committee ever offered an amendment to reduce the tax rates. The rates of the Morgenthau admendment were agreed to by the Ways and Means Committee without a dissenting vote and remained in the bill ever after.*

Benefits. The original bill, following recommendations of the staff, had two benefit schedules: (1) a temporary plan for persons brought under the old age insurance system in the first five years of its existence, and (2) a permanent plan applicable to persons entering the system in 1942 and thereafter. These two plans did not agree with each other, a fact which was discovered shortly before the filing of the report

---

*In the years 1960–1962 the tax rate which applied only to the first $4800 of wages was 3 per cent from the employee and 3 per cent from the employer. The maximum rate is scheduled to be reached in 1969 at 4.5 per cent.—ED.

of the Committee on Economic Security. It was then agreed by everyone actively connected with the committee that the schedules would have to be revised and work was begun on such a revision. Before this was completed, this discrepancy was brought to general public attention by Senator Hastings, who had the assistance of Mr. Foell, a District of Columbia insurance man who had organized the Thrift Foundation, one of the purposes of which organization, apparently, was to fight the social security bill.

The revision of the benefit provisions was included with the change in the tax rate in the Morgenthau amendment. In this revision, all distinction between a temporary and a permanent plan was dropped. The new benefit rates were still geared to average contributions of 5 per cent during an industrial lifetime, but a new principle was introduced to give relatively larger benefits to workers receiving low wages. This idea had been discussed favorably by the staff on old age security, but never had been worked out. It was included in the Morgenthau amendment largely on the insistence of Mr. Reagh, the actuary of the Treasury Department, and was worked out by Mr. Reagh and Mr. Latimer jointly. Like the change in tax rates, also included in the Morgenthau amendment, this revision of the benefit rates was never seriously questioned by any member of either congressional committee.

Exemption of Agriculture and Domestic Service. The staff of the Committee on Economic Security recommended that the old age insurance taxes and benefits be limited to industrial workers, excluding persons engaged in agriculture and domestic service. The Committee on Economic Security struck out this limitation and recommended that the old age insurance system be made applicable to all employed persons. This change was made largely at the insistence of Mr. Hopkins, but was favored also by Secretary Perkins.

152

Subordinate officials in the Treasury, particularly those in charge of internal revenue collections, objected to such inclusive coverage on the score that it would prove administratively impossible to collect payroll taxes from agricultural workers and domestic servants. They persuaded Secretary Morgenthau that the bill must be amended to exclude these groups of workers, to make it administratively feasible. Secretary Morgenthau presented this view in his testimony before the Ways and Means Committee, when he urged adoption of the Morgenthau amendment. Secretary Perkins, who attended the same hearing, when called upon by the committee, endorsed the Morgenthau amendment, but strongly objected to the restriction of coverage.[86]

In the executive sessions of the Ways and Means Committee, the recommendations of Secretary Morgenthau were adopted, practically without dissent. In taking this position, the committee apparently was influenced far less by the difficulties of administration than by the fact that it was felt that the farmers would object to being taxed for old age insurance protection for their employees. Agriculture and domestic service are customarily excluded in this country from all types of laws regulating employment conditions, and the Ways and Means Committee in this instance merely followed established practice. Secretary Perkins was strongly opposed to this amendment, but made no attempt to get it out after it was once inserted in the bill. It was her view that the inclusiveness of coverage was relatively unimpor-

86. This occurrence, in part, explains the misimpression created in newspaper dispatches that the Committee on Economic Security was divided on the Morgenthau amendment. This amendment related to tax rates and benefits and was supported unanimously by the committee. Division existed only over the exclusion of agriculture and domestic service which was not a part of the Morgenthau amendment but an entirely distinct matter, although also urged by Secretary Morgenthau in his appearance before the Ways and Means Committee.

tant, because she felt that the law could easily be amended in later years to afford wider coverage.

Exemption of Charitable, Educational, and Religious Institutions. Much greater differences of opinion developed over another amendment adopted by the Ways and Means Committee, limiting the coverage of the old age insurance system. This was an amendment exempting charitable, educational, religious, etc., organizations from the tax for old age insurance purposes and excluding their employees from old age benefits.

This amendment resulted from objections to the original bill on the part of representatives of the church pension funds. Shortly after the introduction of the bill, the twenty-one church pension funds held a conference at Washington in which they decided to ask Congress for an amendment to exclude churches contributing to church pension funds. An amendment to this effect was presented to both congressional committees by George A. Huggins, Philadelphia, who was the actuary for the Church Pension Conference.

Two of the organizations connected with the Church Fund Conference did not restrict their efforts to this formal presentation of the wishes of this group. These were the Church Pension Fund (of the Episcopal Church) and the Presbyterian Church Pension Fund. Both these organizations sent circular letters to clergymen connected with their churches, including ministers in receipt of retirement allowances. In these letters, the impression was conveyed that the social security bill would compel the abandonment of the church pension funds, and the clergymen to whom they were addressed were invited to write or telegraph protests to their members of Congress. The result was that numerous telegrams and letters of protest were received by members of Congress, particularly those connected with the Ways and Means Committee. Some of these came from retired clergymen who were under the impression that the Social

154

Security Act would result in a termination of their retirement allowances.

Similar requests for exemption from the old age insurance parts of the social security bill were presented to the congressional committees by representatives of the educational institutions of the country and the National Hospital Association. These groups, like the Church Pension Conference, argued that they were dependent very largely upon private charity for support and that they would have to contract their work if they were made subject to the tax for old age security purposes. The Catholic Church did not publicly take the same position, but certain members of the Ways and Means Committee were very much concerned that the Church and all of its charitable enterprises should be exempted.

This matter came up unscheduled in executive session of the Ways and Means Committee when Chairman Doughton read a piteous letter he had received from a retired Presbyterian clergyman. Immediately thereafter a motion was made to exclude from coverage not only the churches having church pension funds, but all charitable, educational, religious, scientific, etc., organizations and their employees. This was adopted without a dissenting vote and was included in the committee's bill as passed by the House.

As soon as this sweeping amendment was adopted, dissent from the action taken developed within the church pension group. This was based upon the fact that many of the churches were on record in favor of the social security legislation and, moreover, none of the church pension funds covered lay workers. A number of people connected with the Church Pension Fund Conference—particularly Mr. Pence of the Young Men's Christian Association, Herman L. Ekern of the Lutheran Brotherhood, and Reverend Wilson of the Christian Church—felt that it was wrong for the churches to advocate old age security and then to deny their

155

own employees the benefits of such security. At the instance of these men, conferences were held, both in Washington and New York, to try to reach an agreement to limit the exclusion of religious and similar organizations which had been included in the social security bill. All but the two church pension funds which had circularized their members against the social security bill wanted a less inclusive exclusion and it is probable that a majority of the funds were willing to have the exclusion stricken out altogether. Mr. Pence particularly was tireless in his efforts to get the amendment relating to the churches either eliminated or much more restricted in scope. He personally called on many of the members of the Senate Finance Committee to tell them that the majority of the Protestant church organizations did not want such an inclusive exclusion. Several drafts of a more restricted exclusion were prepared by Herman L. Ekern and given to members of the Senate committee. In the end, however, no motion to limit this exclusion was even offered in the Senate Finance Committee or on the floor of the Senate. The explanation is that the senators felt uncertain about the attitude of the church groups and did not want to incur the hostility of any of them. This was also the attitude of the Committee on Economic Security throughout all of the many conferences on this particular exclusion (which affected unemployment insurance as well as old age insurance, but was always discussed as if it affected only old age insurance). It was felt that it was up to the church groups to settle among themselves what they wanted in this matter. While the great majority of the representatives of the churches were very positive that they did not want an exclusion which left them in the position of seeming to get a special privilege at the expense of their lay workers, there was always a suspicion that some of the churches wanted the exemption, and neither the committee nor the members of

156

Congress felt that they could afford to incur the enmity of any church group.*

Industrial Pensions. Relatively little attention was paid by the Committee on Economic Security to the relation of existing private pension plans to the compulsory old age insurance system. The members of the old age security staff always made light of possible opposition from employers having industrial pension plans. Mr. Brown and Mr. Latimer talked to some of the men in charge of personnel relations in several large companies having private pension plans and reached the conclusion that they would not object to a compulsory pension system which contained no special provisions for employers with existing industrial pension plans.

When the economic security bill was introduced without any provisions for special treatment to employers with industrial pension plans, some insurance men interested in group annuity insurance came to the Committee on Economic Security to urge an amendment exempting from the taxes for old age insurance purposes employers having industrial pension systems providing at least as liberal benefits as those contemplated in the federal act. Of these, the most aggressive was H. Walter Forster of Towers, Perrin, Forster and Crosby, Inc., Philadelphia, insurance brokers who have specialized in group annuity contracts. Besides Forster, representatives of the Equitable Life Assurance Society, particularly Mr. Horlick and Mr. Hamilton, were active in urging an exemption of employers with industrial pension plans, at least those whose plans were insured by reputable insurance companies.

Forster alone testified before the Ways and Means Com-

*In the years since 1935, Congress has gradually eliminated or narrowed the exclusions from coverage discussed in these several pages. By 1961 virtually all employed and self-workers were covered by some federal retirement program.—ED.

157

mittee and presented a draft of an amendment to exempt employers with industrial pension plans from the tax for old age insurance purposes. This amendment went "the whole hog," containing no safeguards for the old age insurance fund, being evidently intended primarily to serve as a basis for bargaining with the Committee on Economic Security. Numerous conferences were held between these gentlemen and Mr. Latimer, representing the committee, but never led to anything. Mr. Latimer was strongly opposed to any exemption and Forster wanted as wide open an amendment as possible. Initially there was a feeling among the people connected with the committee that some sort of a compromise would have to be worked out, but Latimer and Brown insisted that an industrial pension exemption would destroy the actuarial character of the old age insurance plan and Eliot and Beaman strongly opposed such an exemption on constitutional grounds. In the end, the committee decided to oppose any and all amendments designed to leave out of the general system employers with industrial pension plans.

Forster personally saw every member of the Ways and Means Committee and Horlick and Hamilton at least some of them. Some employers with industrial pension plans wrote their members of Congress protesting against the social security bill on the score that it would compel them to give up their industrial pension plans. Nevertheless, there was relatively little sentiment for exemption of industrial pension systems in the Ways and Means Committee, when this question first came up in the executive sessions. Shortly before the committee made its report, however, the question was revised, when Forster requested that he be permitted to come before the committee to present a new proposal. It was at this stage that the subcommittee headed by Congressman Vinson was created to reexamine the old age insurance titles of the bill. This subcommittee decided to hear Forster in favor of the proposal to exempt employers having industrial pension plans, and Latimer against it. After presentation of these arguments, the subcommittee voted against the industrial pension exemption. Its conclusion was reported back to the full committee and adopted without further discussion. The bill reported by the committee did not include an industrial pension exemption and no attempt was made on the floor to bring this in through amendment.

Retirement. All actuarial calculations were made on the assumption that annuities would be paid only to employees retiring from active employment, and this was provided in the original economic security bill. The only person to object to this provision was Mr. Beaman. He raised the point that "active employment" needed to be defined and rejected every attempted definition. The entire matter was referred to the subcommittee mentioned in the preceding paragraph. This subcommittee, after something like an hour's consideration, in which every suggestion made by anyone to define retirement was rejected by Mr. Beaman as not being sufficiently definite, finally adopted a motion to strike out the provision entirely. It apparently was not realized by anyone that this change would operate to again create a large deficit in the old age insurance fund; in fact, there was no discussion of the financial effects whatsoever. When the subcommittee made its report to the full committee, its recommendation to eliminate the provision relating to retirement was adopted without discussion. As a result, no provision to this effect was included in the House bill.

Senate and Conference Committee Changes

As has been recited, old age insurance was the principal subject of controversy in the deliberations of the Senate Finance Committee on the social security bill. Two major questions were presented: (1) whether the old age insurance titles should remain in the bill at all, and (2) whether employers maintaining industrial pension systems should be exempted from these titles. In addition, the Senate committee gave some attention to the requirement of retirement which was stricken from the original bill by the House committee.

Upon this last point, there was no difference of opinion among the members of the committee. In a public statement given out after passage of the House bill, the President included an item to the effect that retirement, of course, should be a condition of the granting of any annuity. This seemed to be taken for granted by all members of the Senate committee, but nothing was done on this subject until the last meeting of the committee. At that time, Senator La Follette offered an amendment prepared by Mr. Eliot, which had the effect of restoring the requirement that annuities should be granted only to employees while not engaged in work in their customary employment. This amendment was adopted without any dissent. Later on it was quite readily agreed upon by the House conferees, who explained that the House committee had never understood that the amendment eliminating the requirement of retirement completely upset the actuarial calculations.

The struggle over the retention of the old age insurance titles has already been briefly described[87] in the account of the struggle in the Senate Finance Committee over the social security bill. Something has also been said about the industrial pension exemption,[88] but some further account of the Clark amendment seems apropros.

When the House committee acted on the industrial pension amendment suggested by Mr. Forster, this subject had not yet attracted any general interest. I doubt whether there were more than a half-dozen employers who by that time had written members to Congress on such an amend-

87. See Part I, pages 101–103, and Note 65.
88. See Part I, pages 99–107.

ment. When the bill came before the Senate committee for action, however, a very different situation existed in this respect. Forster had circularized all employers known to have industrial pension plans and urged them to demand an exemption. All senators, and particularly those on the Finance Committee, then heard from home, and several members of the committee staunchly supported the proposal to exempt employers with industrial pension systems of their own. Among these was Senator Clark, who became the champion of the industrial pension exemption, which came to be known as the "Clark amendment." Senators George and King likewise strongly favored this amendment.

The Clark amendment was a revised draft of the industrial pension exemption considered in the House. This draft was prepared by Forster and a Mr. Turner, a law partner or a former law partner of Senator Clark. It included some provisions which could be described as protective of the federal old age insurance fund, but which did not adequately protect the fund. This was pointed out to the committee by Mr. Latimer, as well as by Beaman, Eliot, and Wilcox (of the Treasury Department). Senator Clark countered by stating that, if additional safeguards were needed, he would be willing to include them, but the attitude of the people supporting the bill was that no amendment could be drafted providing an exemption for employers with industrial pension plans which would not endanger the entire old age insurance plan. As previously recited, the final vote in committee on the Clark amendment was a tie, with a considerable number of members not recorded. This tie vote kept the amendment out of the bill for the time being, but Senator Clark was successful in securing its adoption on the floor of the Senate, over the strong opposition of the Administration, as well as of organized labor.

The Administration at once let it be known that it did not intend to accept defeat on the Clark amendment as

161

final. The President advised all members of Congress who came to see him about the matter that he would not approve the social security bill unless the Clark amendment was eliminated. In the end, as related, the Administration won out, but only with a compromise under which a special committee was created to try to work out a generally acceptable amendment, accomplishing the purposes of the Clark amendment, for presentation at the next session of Congress.

SECURITY FOR CHILREN

Aid to Dependent Children

The recommendations of the Committee on Economic Security relating to grants-in-aid to states for aid to dependent children (mothers' pensions) were largely based on the report made to the committee by Miss Katherine Lenroot and Dr. Martha Eliott of the United States Children's Bureau. These recommendations contemplated administration by the United States Children's Bureau, and this was taken for granted in all discussions of these recommendations by the technical board and the Committee on Economic Security. In the final stage of the preparation of the committee's report (when the draft of this report which I had prepared was referred by the members of the committee to subordinate officials within their departments), the F.E.R.A. people, particularly Mr. Aubrey J. Williams and Miss Josephine Brown, took the position that aid to dependent children was public assistance and should be administered by the Federal Emergency Relief Administration. Several formal and informal conferences followed, with the final upshot that the committee's report and the original bill provided for administration of the grants-in-aid to the states for aid to dependent children by the Federal Emergency Relief Administrator.

The Ways and Means Committee objected to administration of the aid for dependent children by the F.E.R.A. on the same ground that it objected to administration of the old age assistance grants by this organization. In was unwilling to give the administration of any part of the social security bill to an emergency agency. Accordingly, it unanimously adopted a motion amending this part of the bill to vest the administration of the federal grants in the Social Security Board. After the bill came over to the Senate, it was suggested by representatives of the Department of Labor that the administration should be vested in the United States Children's Bureau. This was discussed briefly in the Senate Finance Committee, but no amendment to make this change ever was offered.

Another important change made from the original bill related to the maximum federal grants for aid to dependent children. In the original bill there was no limitation except that the federal government would not pay more than one-third of the amounts expended by the state and local governments for aid to dependent children. When this part of the bill was reached in the executive sessions of the Ways and Means Committee, the view was expressed by several members that there ought to be a maximum limitation corresponding to the maximum grant of $15 per month in old age assistance. It was then suggested by Congressman Vinson that the limitation should be the same amount as the maximum pension payable to children of servicemen who lost their lives in the [First] World War, namely, $18 per month for the first child and $12 for the second and additional children in the family. In making this suggestion, the congressman completely overlooked the fact that under the Veteran's Pension Act a grant of $30 per month is made to the widow, while in aid for dependent children the grant for the children must normally also provide for the mother who takes care of them. No one pointed out this fact at the time, and Congressman Vinson's motion was adopted without dissent. This fixed the maximum federal aid for dependent children at $6 per month for the first child in any family and $4 for the second and additional children.

After this motion had been adopted, I called the attention of Congressman Vinson and other members of the House committee to the fact that this limitation would operate to keep the federal grants below one-third of the states' expenditures in many cases; further, that it was utterly illogical to expect a mother with a child under sixteen to live on $18 per month when old age assistance grants of $30 per month per person were contemplated in the same act. This was acknowledged to be a justified criticism, but there was so little interest on the part of any of the members in the aid to dependent children that no one thereafter made a motion to strike out the restriction.

Among the amendments which Secretary Perkins, on behalf of the Committee on Economic Security, outlined to the Senate Finance Committee in its first executive session as being very essential was one to strike out the restriction on the aid for dependent children. When it came to action upon the matter, however, Chairman Harrison expressed the view that it probably was all right to start this aid at a very low figure, as subsequent Congresses easily could increase it. A motion was nevertheless made to strike the restriction, but this never came to a formal vote.

There was little interest in Congress in the aid to dependent children. It is my belief that nothing would have been done on this subject if it had not been included in the report of the Committee on Economic Security. That the grants to states for this purpose are limited to one-third of their expenditures, while the grants for old age assistance and blind pensions are for one-half of the expenditures, reflects this complete lack of interest in the aid for dependent children. The one-third figure was suggested by the Children's Bureau because that bureau had previously recommended aid to the states on this basis (which contemplated that federal, state, and local governments should each bear one-third of the costs of this aid). When the aid for old age assistance was fixed at one-half of the costs (which in the Dill-Connery bill of the preceding session was also proposed on a one-third basis), the aid for dependent children should have been changed correspondingly, but those of us who were really interested in this latter aid did not feel that it was wise to raise the point, lest we lose this aid altogether. This was possibly a mistake, but the action of Congress on the amendment limiting the maximum aid per child indicated that there was perhaps some justification for this fear.

Maternal and Child Health

The three other aids concerned with security for children which are included in the Social Security Act had a somewhat similar history, but at all times were considered to fall within the domain of the Children's Bureau.

Of these three aids, the aid for maternal and child health services was the one in which the Children's Bureau was most interested. This aid, in effect, was a revival, increase, and extension of the aid given to the states under the Sheppard-Towner Act, from 1922 to 1929. This aid under the Sheppard-Towner Act was discontinued, partly in an economy streak of Congress and partly because its administration had aroused the opposition of some influential people in the Catholic Church, the United States Public Health Service, and the doctors generally. On the other hand, it was very popular with the women's organizations, which ceaselessly agitated for the renewal of the Sheppard-Towner Act, after discontinuance of the aid in 1929.

Miss Abbott and Miss Lenroot saw a possibility of the renewal of this aid as a part of the social security program and were successful in getting the Committee on Economic Security to agree with them. Then, with consummate skill, they not only worked out the details of their program, but overcame the opposition which had swamped the Sheppard-Towner Act.

The opposition of the Catholics, I believe, was overcome largely through the personal friendly relations which Miss Lenroot had developed with Father (later Monsignor) O'Grady, the unofficial legislative representative of the Catholic Church in Washington. The opposition of the doctors was largely nullified through the fact that the Committee on Economic Security at the same time recommended increased appropriations to the United States Public Health Service. This committee helped greatly to establish more friendly relations between the United States Public Health Service and the Children's Bureau. Dr. Sydenstricker, the consulting statistician of the United States Public Health Service, had charge of the health studies of the committee; Miss Lenroot, of the studies relating to security for children. Between them, they agreed upon a program under which the Children's Bureau was to administer the aids for maternal and child health services, but with provisions insuring consultation with the doctors. The Advisory Medical Committee mildly protested against permitting the Children's Bureau to control the maternal and child health services and the American Medical Association, at a special delegate convention held in Chicago in February, 1935, adopted a resolution vigorously condemning this proposal for "lay control of medicine," but neither group did anything further on this matter.

When the President was advised of the recommendations to be made by the Committee on Economic Security, he stated that the aid for maternal and child health services might meet the bitter opposition of the Catholics. He nevertheless was willing to go along with this recommendation of the committee. In the committee's presentation of the economic security bill in the congressional hearings, some effort

166

was made to distinguish the recommendations from the Sheppard-Towner Act, but this was not very successful. The members of Congress always spoke of the aid for maternal and child health as a renewal of the Sheppard-Towner Act, and acted with this concept in mind.

Anticipated opposition to this aid, however, never materialized, at least on any serious scale. Some Catholics were suspicious of the provision, but the Church offered no opposition to the proposal. Father O'Grady and several other prominent Catholics did very effective work in support of the economic security bill as a whole and never voiced any of the fears which, possibly, they may have entertained regarding this particular title. The American Medical Association was far too alarmed about the possibility of health insurance to present any very serious objection to the administration of the child and maternal health services through the Children's Bureau. The United States Public Health Service made no objection whatsoever and loyally supported the entire economic security bill. All of the leading women's organizations of the country were represented at the congressional hearings to express their peculiar interest in this and the other aids relating to security for children. The net result was that the aid for maternal and child health services was never once questioned in the executive sessions of the congressional committees or during the debate in the two houses.

Child Welfare Services

The authorized aid of $1,500,000 per year for state and local welfare services, which appears in Part (3) of Title V of the Social Security Act, was a new departure suggested by the Children's Bureau. It was approved by the technical board and the Committee on Economic Security without much special consideration. It was included in the original economic security bill on the same basis as the other two aids dealt with in this section. This included a matching by the state and local governments of the federal aid, dollar for dollar, and the submission and approval of a state plan providing methods of administration satisfactory to the Children's Bureau and also providing for financial participation by the state government.

No sooner had the report of the Committee on Economic Security gone in and the economic security bill been introduced when it developed that these conditions were very objectionable to the Catholics with whom the committee was in touch. Their objection was first put in terms of a fear that this plan would involve federal and state control of church and other private charitable institutions concerned with child welfare. Soon it developed that there was another factor, namely, that public (local) money is paid in certain metropolitan centers (New York, Chicago, Philadelphia, Pittsburgh, and perhaps others) to charitable institutions conducted by religious groups for the care in these institutions of children committeed to their custody by courts. It was feared that either the state or federal authorities might object to these arrangements made by local authorities, and this fear was, perhaps, the major reason for opposition to the conditions governing this aid which were included in the original bill.

The Catholic opposition was revealed in protests to the President, to Secretary Perkins, and to the committee itself. In an attempt to allay this opposition, I arranged a conference, through Father O'Grady, with interested representatives of the Catholic institutions. This was attended by some six to ten persons prominent in Catholic welfare work, including Father O'Grady, Monsignor Wagner (then the President of the National Catholic Welfare Conference), and Father Butler (a later President of this organization). Mr. Eliot, Miss Lenroot, and I were the only representatives of the Committee on Economic Security, and we spent several hours going over the entire matter.

This was one of the most successful of all conferences in which I participated during the entire period of the development of the Social Security Act. We, the representatives of the committee, had not been aware of the possible interference with local arrangements affecting the charitable institutions conducted by religious organizations and, of course, had no intention of interfering with the arrangements. Consequently, we offered to accept any revision of the provisions of this particular part of the bill which would be acceptable to the Church representatives. What they asked was that the requirement for the matching of the federal aid be dropped; also, the requirement of state financial participation; further, they urged that this federal aid be limited to rural areas in which there are no adequate provisions for child welfare services. This latter suggestion was in accord with the report of the Committee on Economic Security, which advanced the lack of adequate child welfare services in rural areas as the reason that federal aid was needed. These suggestions of the representatives of the Catholic Church were accepted by us, with the understanding that they would not object to any other part of the bill and would actively support the measure.

The agreement reached in this conference was faithfully carried out. The matter was not discussed in the congressional hearings at all, but when this particular provision was reached in the executive sessions of the Ways and Means Committee an amendment was offered by Congressman McCormack changing these sections in accord with the Catholic wishes. Being called upon to comment, I stated that the Committee on Economic Security was entirely agreeable to this amendment and explained the reasons it was deemed necessary by the Catholics. The Ways and Means Committee wrangled for some time over what should be considered a

169

rural area and adopted somewhat more restrictive language upon this point than provided for in the McCormack amendment. Thereafter, the amendment was adopted without objection. In the Senate, Senator Gerry questioned the adequacy of the amendment and some slight verbal changes were made to make sure that it conferred no control over private charitable institutions upon either state or federal authorities.

Leading Catholics, on their part, actively supported the economic security bill subsequent to the conference referred to. Some questions were raised regarding the parts of the bill relating to maternal and child health services and crippled children's services, on much the same grounds as there had been objection to the original version of the aid for child welfare services. Father O'Grady answered these objections for us by calling attention to the fact that his group had agreed to support the bill if the section on the aid for child welfare services was modified as agreed upon. Father O'Grady was in close touch with many members of Congress and proved one of the most valuable supporters of the bill. It is my belief that he influenced a great many members of Congress to support the bill who otherwise would have opposed it.

Besides this major revision, this part of the social security bill was subjected to many verbal changes. Mr. Beaman insisted that "child welfare services" had no defined meaning and many members of the Ways and Means Committee seemed to have no conception of what was meant by the term. To meet these objections, I suggested the definition which occurs in the final act.* This was not altogether acceptable to Mr. Beaman, but was adopted in lieu of any other

* Section 521(a) includes the following phrase: ". . . public-welfare services (hereinafter in this section referred to as 'child-welfare services') for the protection and care of homeless, dependent, and neglected children, and children in danger of becoming delinquent."—ED.

better definition. What constituted "rural areas" was also very much debated, but the committee was finally satisfied with "predominantly rural areas."

Crippled Children's Services

The aid to states for crippled children's services at no stage involved any serious difficulties. This aid was suggested by the Children's Bureau, in part, because it was thought that President Roosevelt would be peculiarly interested in it. He approved the aid without question, but never manifested any greater interest in this particular aid than in any other provision of the social security bill.

In the congressional hearings and executive sessions, the aid for crippled children's services was never really questioned. The only comments made related to the fact that many private groups, particularly the Shriners and the Children's Fund of Michigan, were doing notable work in this field. It was agreed, however, that there was also need for state activity and that it was desirable for the federal government to encourage the states to undertake a comprehensive program of services for crippled children.

PUBLIC HEALTH WORK

The authorized appropriations for public health work in Title VI of the final act were throughout the congressional consideration of this measure a source of strength for the bill. The aids provided in this title were understood to be primarily for states in which public health work had been backward, due largely to state proverty. These were particularly the southern states, and the heads of the state departments of health in nearly all these states appeared before the congressional committees to endorse this part of the bill. They gave very strong testimony regarding the need for additional public health work in the South and

171

these arguments strongly appealed to members of Congress from this section, many of whom were very influential in the two committees considering this legislation.

Public health work was not originally thought of in connection with economic security. As previously recited, the committee early in its history employed Dr. Edgar L. Sydenstricker to head its studies in the health field, and he associated with himself Dr. I. S. Falk. These studies were thought of by the committee and by Doctors Sydenstricker and Falk as being concerned principally with health insurance. The first person who suggested that they should be broadened to include public health services was Dr. Michael M. Davis, director of the medical activities of the Julius Rosenwald Fund. The same view was shortly after expressed by the subcommittee on health problems of the technical board, which reviewed the tentative recommendations presented by Doctors Sydenstricker and Falk in connection with the preliminary report of the staff. Thereafter, the studies of the staff in this field were broadened to include public health and medical services, several specialists being employed to assist Doctors Sydenstricker and Falk in this field.

In the first meetings of the Medical Advisory Committee, and of the other advisory committees in the public health field, which were held in the last weeks of November, Doctors Sydenstricker and Falk presented recommendations dealing not only with health insurance, but with increased federal appropriations for public health work, to be devoted to an expansion of the United States Public Health Service and to aid to the states for state and local public health services. These recommendations met a favorable response from all of the advisory committees,[89] and were specifically en-

89. Some of the members of the Medical Advisory Committee believed that much more good could be accomplished through an extension of public health work and public medical services than through health insurance, while a somewhat larger group, who were strongly

172

dorsed by the American Medical Association in its special delegate meeting held at Chicago in February, 1935.

Throughout the consideration of this part of the bill, no one ever objected to the public health appropriations. In its original form, this title was drafted to suit the wishes of the United States Public Health Service. Two million dollars was authorized to be appropriated directly to the Public Health Service for the extension of its staff, while $8,000,000 was allotted for aid to the states for strengthening state and local public health services. This aid was left entirely within the control of the Public Health Service, it being given authority to allot the money between the states as it deemed necessary.

This was the broadest grant of discretion occurring in any part of the economic security bill. No questions regarding this delegation of broad discretion, however, were raised until near the end of the executive sessions of the Ways and Means Committee. An amendment was then offered and adopted somewhat limiting this discretion. This became a part of the final act, but this title still vests broader discretionary power in the United States Public Health Service than is conferred upon any federal agency in any other title.

HEALTH INSURANCE

Developments Prior to the First Meetings of the Medical Advisory Committee

No provisions relating to health insurance (other than for further study of the problem) were ever included in the social security bill at any stage; the subject received only brief treatment in the report of the Committee on Economic Security; nevertheless, this was a subject to which the

---

opposed to health insurance, looked upon increased appropriations for public health work as a means of killing the proposal for health insurance.

Committee on Economic Security had to devote a great deal of attention.

Any comprehensive survey of the social insurance field, such as was indicated in the President's message of June 8, 1934, necessarily had to include health insurance. It was my original belief, however, that it would probably be impossible to do anything about health insurance in a legislative way, due to the expected strong opposition of the medical profession. I found that this was, also, the view of Secretary Perkins and Dr. Altmeyer, whose primary interest was in unemployment insurance. Mr. Hopkins was more interested in health insurance than in any other phase of social insurance, but also realized that this subject would have to be handled very gingerly.

It was taken for granted by everyone connected with the committee that a study of health insurance would be included among its research studies. Dr. Edgar L. Sydenstricker was the person everyone agreed best qualified to make this study, and he associated with himself his principal associate in the Research Department of the Milbank Memorial Fund, Dr. I. S. Falk. An announcement of this study was included in the first newspaper story given out about the research work to be undertaken by the Committee on Economic Security, about the middle of August. As soon as this announcement was made (along with a long list of other studies to be undertaken), telegraphic protests poured in upon the President. In the *Journal of the American Medical Association*, an editorial was run in which it was stated that the Administration, acting through the Committee on Economic Security, would try to railroad health insurance through Congress, without as much as consulting the profession, and similar comments were made in several of the official publications of state medical associations. These attacks led the President to take a personal interest in this matter. He directed his personal physician, Dr. McIntyre

174

(a naval officer), to keep in touch with the Committee on Economic Security on the development of this particular part of its program. Throughout the time I was connected with the committee, I (and also Dr. Sydenstricker and Dr. Falk) had many conferences with Dr. McIntyre at the White House and through him communicated frequently with the President on matters concerned with health insurance.

At the very outset, Dr. Sydenstricker discussed the advisability of a professional advisory committee to assist the staff in working out the health insurance program. When the American Medical Association launched its attacks upon the committee, the organization of such an advisory committee was also strongly urged by Dr. McIntyre. That such an advisory committee would be organized was announced publicly in a letter which I wrote to the American Medical Association, in reply to its hostile editorial. The selection of this advisory committee was made with great care. The initial suggestions for the members of this committee were made by Doctors Sydenstricker and Falk and then taken by me to Dr. McIntyre to be presented to the President.[90] Dr. McIntyre was anxious to get very eminent members of the profession who would approach the problem of health insurance fairly and command general confidence. He was anxious to avoid any persons who had committed themselves one way or the other on the question, or at least a preponderance of such persons. Considerable attention was also given to geographic distribution, to give some representation to every section of the country. The major medical organizations were not asked to make nominations, but it was deemed advisable to appoint to the committee the

90. Several of the members of the Medical Advisory Committee were first suggested by Dr. McIntyre or the President, among them Drs. Cushing, Crile, and Parran. The President also suggested Dr. Mayo, and it was at his instance that the attempt was made to get Dr. Mayo to accept the chairmanship of the committee.

presidents of the American Medical Association, the American College of Surgeons, and the American College of Physicians.[91]

For chairman of the Medical Advisory Committee, the President was anxious to secure Dr. Willam Mayo, but he declined on the ground of his advanced age. An attempt was then made to get Dr. Minot of Harvard University to serve, but he had to go to Sweden to receive the Nobel Prize he had just been awarded. In the end, no chairman was designated either of this committee or of any other advisory committee in the health field. This was Dr. Sydenstricker's idea, being grounded in a fear that the selection of a chairman would lead to involvement in medical politics.

Three other advisory committees in this field were announced simultaneously with the Medical Advisory Committee. These were the Public Health Advisory Committee, the Hospital Advisory Committee, and the Dental Advisory Committee; and later (in January), a Nurses' Advisory Committee was organized. The selection of none of these committees created any particular difficulty and they never assumed the importance of the Medical Advisory Committee. After these committees were announced, several other organizations in the health field protested that they had been ignored, among them the Chiropractors, the Osteopaths, the National Medical Association (a Negro organization), and the Homeopaths. None of these groups could be given representation without seriously offending the major medical

91. In the case of the American College of Physicians, the vice-president was appointed rather than the president, because the latter was a Canadian.

The suggestion that the presidents of the three major medical associations be appointed to the Medical Advisory Committee was first made by Dr. Franklin H. Martin, director general of the American College of Surgeons, a close friend of the President. It was accepted as a way of making certain that the American Medical Association could not claim that it was not represented, without asking it to nominate any persons for membership on the committee.

organizations. They, consequently, had to be left out, although the Homeopaths had as their spokesman Senator Copeland, a member of their organization.

Despite the care with which the Medical Advisory Committee was selected, it drew instant fire from groups close to the inner circle of the American Medical Association. The list of the members of this committee was carried in the newspapers of the first Sunday of November. Before midnight of that day, scores of telegrams had poured in upon the President, principally from physicians in Pennsylvania and Ohio, protesting that no general practitioner had been named as a member of the committee. Even before the committee was announced, telegrams were received from Colorado, Wyoming, and neighboring Rocky Mountain states, protesting that no person from the Rocky Mountain area had been selected for membership and suggesting a Denver physician who was an outspoken opponent of health insurance. Other telegrams protested the alleged unfairness of the Committee on Economic Security and its staff. Literally hundreds of telegrams of this vein were sent to the President or to members of the committee, generally in batches from a particular section of the country and often identical in wording. Similarly, numerous articles attacking the committee were published in medical journals throughout the country.

Developments at the First Meetings
of the Medical Advisory Committee

This situation continued until the first meetings of the Medical Advisory Committee, which were held in the two days following the National Conference on Economic Security. Thereafter, the attacks upon the committee stopped very suddenly, as did the telegrams to the President. The explanation of this phenomena lay in occurrences during the National Conference on Economic Security and the first meetings of the Medical Advisory Committee.

A roundtable on medical care was included in the program of the National Conference on Economic Security. Of the four speakers selected to lead this discussion at this roundtable, two were known advocates of health insurance and two strong opponents. These discussion leaders were selected by Dr. Sydenstricker because of their known views on this very controversial subject, the intention being that both sides should be presented, without any indication from the committee which it would favor. As it turned out, one of the speakers expected to support health insurance (Dr. Luce of Detroit) actually delivered a speech very critical of this institution. At this session an unfortunate colloquy occurred between Dr. Michael M. Davis and Dr. Cushing, which suggested a very hostile attitude on the part of the latter[92] towards health insurance and seemed to foreshadow a wide-open split over this issue on the Medical Advisory Committee.

A more friendly attitude was created by the speech of Secretary Perkins at the dinner which concluded the National Conference, in which the Secretary expressed understanding with the disturbed attitude of the doctors and her faith that they would act on the new problems with which they were faced in accordance with the traditional high ideals of their profession. In her opening address at the first meeting of the Medical Advisory Committee on the next day, she added that the Committee on Economic Security had no intention of railroading any proposition and recognized that the Medical Advisory Committee probably could not complete its work by December 1, and that, if it

92. On the day of the National Conference, Dr. Cushing had lunch with the President and on the next day he took a much more friendly attitude toward the Committee on Economic Security and continued of this mood until after the committee endorsed compulsory health insurance in principle in its report in January.

asked for an extension of time, the committee would be glad to accede to its request.

Most important in bringing about a better attitude on the part of the medical organizations, however, were the developments at these first meetings of the Medical Advisory Committee. Discussion at these meetings centered far less around the tentative recommendations made by Doctors Sydenstricker and Falk than upon the attitude of the American Medical Association and the subject of health insurance. With Dr. Bierring, the President of the American Medical Association sitting as a member, and Dr. Leland and Mr. Simons of its Bureau of Medical Economics of the American Medical Association in attendance at the express invitation of Dr. Sydenstricker, several members of the Medical Advisory Committee sharply criticized the American Medical Association for its narrow attitude on the subject of health insurance. The climax came when Dr. Bruce, a member of the Medical Advisory Committee, presented what he believed to be evidence that the American Medical Association had been responsible for the remarkable change in position manifested by Dr. Luce in his speech at the National Conference on Economic Security the preceding day.[93] The final upshot of the entire discussion was that Dr. Cushing, as well as several members of the committee who were more favorably inclined towards health insurance, pointedly told Dr. Bierring that tactics of this sort must stop or that the American Medical Association would be split wide open. Dr. Bierring gave assurance that the American Medical Association would change its attitude and would be willing to work with the

93. This evidence was to the effect that Dr. Luce had been subjected to something akin to a boycott when he made his report to the Michigan State Medical Association, that when he was announced as one of the speakers at the National Conference on Economic Security he was visited by a representative from the Chicago office of the American Medical Association and given to understand that he might get back into good standing by reversing his position.

Medical Advisory Committee and the Committee on Economic Security in trying to reach a generally acceptable solution.

This promise was fulfilled in good faith by the American Medical Association. Following the meeting of the Medical Advisory Committee, Dr. Fishbein, the editor of the *Journal of the American Medical Association,* called me by long-distance telephone to read an editorial he had written, expressing confidence in the Committee on Economic Security and the Advisory Medical Committee. For some time thereafter there were cordial relations between our committee and the American Medical Association. These included an agreement that Dr. Leland and Mr. Simons would work with Doctors Sydenstricker and Falk in developing their recommendations more in detail.

This truce was interpreted by the Committee on Economic Security as indicating a possibility that a program for health insurance reasonably acceptable to the medical profession might be worked out, or at least that the entire Medical Advisory Committee (with the possible exception of Dr. Bierring) might be willing to get behind such a program. This belief was strengthened by the fact that the American College of Surgeons definitely came out for health insurance at its Boston meeting held shortly before the National Conference on Economic Security. As events developed, subsequently, it now seems to me that this optimistic view misinterpreted the attitude of the important members of the Medical Advisory Committee. Talks which I subsequently had with Doctors Cushing, Bierring, Greenough, and Crile, as well as with a number of physicians not members of the Medical Advisory Committee, led me to believe the conciliatory attitude which was developed at the first of the meetings of the Medical Advisory Committee was due far more to a desire to stop the controversy within the medical profession over health insurance than to any more favorable

180

attitude towards its establishment. Several of the members of the Medical Advisory Committee were very much concerned about the division in the profession over health insurance, which had come to the fore since the Committee on Cost of Medical Care was organized in 1927. These members did not believe in health insurance and were unwilling to endorse it in any form, but they were anxious to heal the split in the medical profession over this issue.[94]

Health Insurance in the Report of Committee

Throughout December and until the report of the Committee on Economic Security was transmitted to the Congress on January 17, there appeared to be every reason to hope that a health insurance program might be worked out which would be accepted by the Medical Advisory Committee, and, perhaps, the American Medical Association. The Medical Advisory Committee, following the suggestion made by Secretary Perkins, asked for additional time to complete its recommendations. An extension until March 1 was then formally granted. This was necessary, in any event, because Doctors Sydenstricker and Falk had not refined their proposals sufficiently to draft any sort of a bill on the subject. At the time, they and all others connected with the Committee on Economic Security thought it advisable to keep health insurance out of the picture until the other recommendations of the committee had been enacted into law. It

94. In the first meetings of the Medical Advisory Committee, Dr. Cushing strongly urged this committee to come out for the establishment of a Cabinet Department of Public Health, arguing that such a department then could work out a program for health insurance acceptable to the profession. Later he strongly supported Dr. Parran in his position that the extension of public medical services was much more promising than health insurance.

In private conversation in March, Dr. Greenough expressed the same general attitude, although a few months before he had endorsed health insurance in his speech as president of the American College of Surgeons.

was anticipated that the economic security bill would be passed early in the coming congressional session and it was thought that thereafter the committee could put in a second report recommending health insurance, which might still be acted upon before the adjournment of Congress.

While not prepared to make definite recommendations on health insurance, Doctors Sydenstricker and Falk deemed it advisable to say something on the subject in the committee's report which would suggest that a health insurance program was coming. They persuaded the committee to include in its report the section on health insurance which appears on pages 41 to 43 of the published report. This was little more than an announcement that the committee expected to make a further report on health insurance, but included language which suggested that the committee would recommend the enactment of legislation on this subject. This was included, in accord with Dr. Sydenstricker's belief that, if the committee announced the principles on which it thought health insurance should be developed, much of the opposition of the doctors would disappear.

Actually, the publication of the committee's report aroused a great furore in the official circles of the American Medical Association. In the medical journals, the committee's recommendations were described as an endorsement of health insurance and many doctors got the impression that the economic security bill included health insurance. In fact, the only reference to health insurance in the entire bill occurred in the enumeration of the duties of the Social Security Board, which included, among the various aspects of social security to be studied by the board, health insurance; but this was sufficient, plus the discussion of the subject in the report of the committee, to once more bring down upon it the full wrath of the opposition to health insurance. A special meeting of the House of Delegates of the American Medical Association was convened in Chicago in the middle of February, 1935. This was the first special meeting of the House of Delegates since the World War. At this meeting, health insurance and the recommendations of the Committee on Economic Security were the only subjects for discussion. The proceedings of the House of Delegates were largely conducted in secret, but the newspapers carried reports of very bitter criticisms of the economic security bill by the doctors. Formal resolutions were adopted endorsing the sections of the bill dealing with increased appropriations for public health work and criticizing those relating to the administration of maternal and child health services by the Children's Bureau. More important were the resolutions redefining the position of the American Medical Association on health insurance. In these resolutions, it reversed its prior position of complete opposition to all forms of health insurance, endorsing instead experimentation with voluntary plans under the control of the county and state medical associations. It strongly condemned compulsory health insurance and all forms of lay control of medicine. In effect, thus, the American Medical Association endorsed voluntary health insurance, but continued its policy of bitter opposition to compulsory health insurance.

This program was effectively calculated to unify the medical profession in opposition to compulsory health insurance. A considerable number of forward-looking men in the profession continued to express their belief that the American Medical Association should participate in the development of a program for compulsory health insurance, whose adoption they believed inevitable. Important groups which a little earlier were inclined to take the same position, however, were disarmed by the apparent change of front of the American Medical Association and considered the program it now recommended as being entitled to a fair trial. Typical was the apparent change of attitude of the American College of Surgeons. While this organization in 1934 came

183

out strongly for health insurance, it completely ignored the subject in its 1935 convention,[95] and the same change occurred in the attitude of the Michigan State Medical Association.[96]

The change of front of the American Medical Association and the effect which this change had in unifying the doctors in opposition to compulsory health insurance, plus the fears which this opposition aroused in Congress, doomed all hopes for early enactment of health insurance legislation. How Congress reacted was demonstrated at the first executive session of the Ways and Means Committee held after the convening of the first meeting of the House of Delegates. This occurred on the morning of the announcement of the attack made upon the economic security bill at this meeting of the House of Delegates in Chicago. Members of the committee wanted to know where health insurance was provided for in the bill. They were told, as they had been many times

95. The change in the attitude of the American College of Surgeons, I believe, was at least in part due to the death of its founder and long its director-general, Dr. Franklin H. Martin, shortly after the special meeting of the House of Delegates of the American Medical Association. With his death, there passed from the scene probably the most influential man in the profession who had come to be convinced that compulsory health insurance was inevitable. Prior to his death, there had been undercover attempts to get him out of his position and to get the College of Surgeons to back down on its endorsement of compulsory health insurance. After his death, the latter proved very easy.

96. The California State Medical Association held a meeting shortly after the change of position of the American Medical Association, at which it refused to be bound by the decision of the House of Delegates and endorsed compulsory health insurance. The bill for health insurance which it supported, however, was one not very objectionable to the American Medical Association and its endorsement of such legislation seems to have been influenced fully as much by the fact that the California legislature appeared to be on the verge of passing some compulsory health insurance bill as by any difference from the point of view of the American Medical Association.

184

before, that the bill contained no provisions for health insurance, but also that the subject was mentioned in the clause already referred to, making it the duty of the Social Security Board to study aspects of social security not dealt with in the bill, including health insurance. A motion was then promptly made to strike out this reference to health insurance and this was adopted unanimously. Time and again thereafter members of Congress received protests from medical associations and individual physicians against the economic security bill, all based on the assumption that this bill provided for health insurance. These required many explanations on our part and invariably the members made it clear that they would have nothing to do with the bill if it contemplated health insurance.[97]

Second Set of Meetings of the Advisory Committee

The Advisory Medical Committee held its second set of meetings in the last days of January, and the other advisory committees in the public health field in the weeks following in February. At these meetings, Doctors Sydenstricker and Falk presented a complete program for health insurance, as well as recommendations for federal aid for some types of public medical services. This program had been submitted in advance to Messrs. Leland and Simons, in accordance with the agreement reached at the first meetings of the Medical Advisory Committee. These representatives of the American Medical Association differed from our staff only upon a few of the details, but continued to take the attitude that compulsory health insurance was inadvisable.

In the consideration of these recommendations by the

97. A health insurance bill, drafted by the Association for Social Security, was introduced by Senator Black. This did not have any Administration support and never even came to a hearing; but in the medical journals this was often identified as a part of the social security program.

185

Advisory Medical Committee, some heated discussion developed between Dr. Cushing and Dr. Sydenstricker, but the latter, with great skill, avoided an open split. Throughout, Dr. Sydenstricker took the position that the Medical Advisory Committee should pass upon only the details of the program, as it was the function of the Committee on Economic Security and the President to decide matters of policy. On the details there were only minor objections to any of the recommendations, and no vote was ever taken on the policy of health insurance. Had such a vote been taken, it probably would have been favorable to health insurance, but only by a divided committee. In his report to the Committee on Economic Security, Dr. Sydenstricker honestly and frankly reported that, while the Medical Advisory Committee and the other advisory committees in the health field had all gone over his recommendations and were satisfied with all details, they had not passed upon the general policy involved.

This set of meetings of the Medical Advisory Committee left several of the members of that committee with a feeling of pronounced hostility. This was particularly true of Dr. Cushing, who transmitted his impressions to the President and protested in writing to the Committee on Economic Security about the alleged unfairness of Dr. Sydenstricker. Statements to this effect were also made at the special meeting of the House of Delegates of the American Medical Association, in which portions of the confidential minutes of the Advisory Medical Committee were read to the entire group of delegates. The members of the advisory committee who entertained these feelings were clearly a minority, but included all those who were close to the inner circle of the American Medical Association. In none of the other advisory committees did any similar difficulties develop, but these committees were very much overshadowed by the Advisory Medical Committee.

186

Report of the Committee on Economic Security on Health Insurance

Regardless of these difficulties and the position taken by the House of Delegates of the American Medical Association, Doctors Sydenstricker and Falk proceeded with the completion of their report and also prepared a draft of a second report to be made by the Committee on Economic Security to the President on the subject of medical care, dealing principally with health insurance.

The time limit set for this second report in the first report of the committee was March 1. By that date, Doctors Sydenstricker and Falk were not quite ready with their final recommendations, but some weeks later they presented these at a meeting of the Committee on Economic Security. They recommended that the economic security bill be amended to include provisions for health insurance. They suggested the levying of an additional tax upon employers against which a credit should be allowed for contributions made to state health insurance funds established under approved state laws. They also suggested supplemental appropriations from general revenues to aid the states in providing adequate medical services, under a compulsory health insurance scheme, for people in the lowest-income groups.

These recommendations met with favorable response on the part of the members of the Committee on Economic Security. Mr. Hopkins always was of the opinion that health insurance was by far the most valuable form of social insurance. Miss Perkins likewise believed in health insurance, although originally she was doubtful whether it was immediately feasible. Secretaries Wallace and Morgenthau at this stage did not attend any meetings of the committee, being represented by Mr. Tugwell and Miss Roche, respectively. Mr. Tugwell was dissatisfied with the economic security bill because it did not go far enough; Miss Roche very ardently favored health insurance and like Dr. Sydenstricker believed that an amendment including health insurance would gain additional support for the bill. Mr. Eliot and I, believing that such an amendment as Dr. Sydenstricker advocated would spell defeat for the entire bill, strongly opposed any report in favor of health insurance before Congress had disposed of the pending bill. At this stage, I indirectly consulted the President, through Dr. McIntyre, and was advised that it was his view that it would be very unwise to throw health insurance into the hopper while the rest of the program was still before Congress. I then strongly urged that the committee should adopt the same policy which it had pursued in relation to its first report, namely that of consulting the President in advance of the filing of any formal recommendations. This had been the universal practice in the current Administration and the suggestion was accepted at once by the committee as the correct procedure. It was decided that Miss Perkins and Miss Roche should confer with the President. They did so and were told to file the report in favor of compulsory health insurance which the committee had in mind, but that the President wanted to determine what should be done with it.

This procedure was followed, although every member of the committee understood that it meant that the President did not intend to come out for health insurance so long as the economic security bill was pending; also, that he had not definitely made up his mind what action he would finally recommend on this subject. Under the circumstances, Doctors Sydenstricker and Falk took their time in completing their report. The report to the President on health insurance, signed by all members of the committee, was filed toward the end of June and the staff report upon which it was presumably based was not finally completed until some time later.

No publicity whatsoever was given to the committee's report on health insurance [see Appendix III] and the fact that such a report was made has never been publicized in the newspapers. When the Social Security Board was organized, the President sent this report to the new board, with a suggestion that it give further study to the subject.

VOCATIONAL REHABILITATION

The problems of the disabled were never given any real consideration by the Committee on Economic Security. Miss Olga S. Halsey of the staff made two reports on invalidity insurance, which was studied because it is a recognized form of social insurance. The technical board discussed this subject and reached the conclusion that invalidity insurance is the most difficult of all forms of social insurance and should, therefore, be considered as one of the items to come last in a complete program for economic security. Some suggestions were made to the committee by the National Council for the Physically Handicapped, and it was always recognized that the care and rehabilitation of the disabled deserved consideration in any complete program for economic security. It was felt, however, that the Committee on Economic Security did not need to deal with the subject, because the federal government was already giving aid for vocational rehabilitation.

In December, when the report of the committee had been all but completed, Mr. Kurtz and Miss Copp, of the Bureau of Vocational Rehabilitation of the Office of Education, called upon me to urge that the committee include in its report a brief statement recognizing the value of the work being done in this field. I did this in the paragraphs in the report devoted to "Educational and Rehabilitation Services," which were accepted by the committee without question. In these paragraphs the committee merely expressed its view that vocational rehabilitation is an important aspect of the problem of economic security and stated that the work already being done in this field should be continued.

No one at this stage suggested that the economic security bill should include any provisions relating to vocational rehabilitation. When it came to the congressional hearings, however, Mr. Studebaker, the United States Commissioner of Education, appeared to urge an amendment authorizing increased appropriations to the Office of Education for federal aid for vocational rehabilitation. At the same time a considerable number of telegrams and letters were sent to the members of the committee urging increased aid for vocational rehabilitation.

We (the people connected with the Committee on Economic Security) were surprised at these tactics, but when asked about the matter had to say that increased appropriations for this purpose were probably justified. Even then we did not think that Congress would do anything along this line. It developed, however, that Congressman Woodruff of the Ways and Means Committee was very much interested in vocational rehabilitation. On his motion, the committee decided to include the amendment suggested by Mr. Studebaker. This was inserted without any opposition and remained in the bill thereafter, without being questioned or discussed.

Mr. Studebaker also suggested an amendment to the bill giving control of the work to be done for crippled children to the Office of Education. This proposal was discussed in both congressional committees, but apparently was not favored by any member.

BLIND PENSIONS

The programs of the blind were regarded by the Committee on Economic Security as falling within a broad general program for economic security, but as not being very immediate.

190

No persons representing any organization for the blind consulted the committee prior to its report and no studies were undertaken in this field by any member of the staff.

When the economic security bill was introduced, several groups interested in the blind consulted the committee and also the members of the congressional committees to whom this bill was referred. A formal suggestion for amendments to include provisions for the blind was made by Mr. Robert B. Irwin of the American Foundation for the Blind. These amendments proposed grants-in-aid to the states for field work for the blind. Mr. Irwin and the other spokesmen for the blind organizations all took the position that the blind pension laws of the states were of doubtful value, but that the federal government should give aid to the states for increased field services to the blind, designed to make as many of the blind self-supporting as possible.

In the Ways and Means Committee, the question of including provisions for the blind was only briefly considered. Without a formal vote, it was decided to do nothing on the subject.

In the Senate Finance Committee, a different attitude was taken. All members seemed to be agreed that something should be done for the blind, but the view was also expressed that field work for the blind meant merely increased employment for social workers. What the committee decided to do was to include in the bill aid to the states for blind pensions, on the same basis as for old age pensions. I was instructed to get information for the committee on the costs of such a program, which I hurriedly did in a brief report furnished all members of the committee. It was on the basis of this report that the appropriation for blind pensions included in the final act was fixed and that the committee made the factual statements on this problem which were included in its report to the Senate.

When the bill came up on the Senate floor, Senator Wagner presented an amendment which he stated had been given to him by Miss Helen Keller to the effect that the states be authorized to spend one-half of the amount received as federal aid under this title for the expansion of their field services for the blind, leaving the other half available only for blind pensions, to be matched from state and local funds. This amendment was adopted without objection and without any discussion of the problem involved, apparently because desired by Miss Keller and offered by Senator Wagner.

In the conference committee, the House members quite readily acceded to the original amendment of the Senate Finance Committee giving federal aid for blind pensions, but made the same objection which had been raised in the Senate Finance Committee for aid for field work for the blind— namely, that such aid benefited social workers rather than the blind. The Senate conferees were of much the same view, so that an agreement was easily reached between the houses. This provided for federal aid for blind pensions, but struck out the Wagner amendment, under which a part of this aid might have been used for field work for the blind.

ADMINISTRATION

The members of the Committee on Economic Security, the members of the technical board, and the executive director all held administrative positions and fully appreciated that the success of any program for economic security depended primarily upon administration. Circumstances were such, however, that the first task of the committee was to formulate and secure the passage of a legislative program. As the committee had but little time to work out this program, however, it was not possible to give as much attention to administrative problems as would have been desirable.

Some studies made for the committee related to these

problems, particularly that of Miss Clark on federal-state relationships, those of Messrs. Harris and Shipman on the deposit of state unemployment compensation funds in the United States Treasury, and the memoranda of Dr. Stewart and Mr. Murray on the stamp book versus the payroll method of collecting unemployment compensation contributions. Similarly, some attention was given to problems of administration in all of the major final reports of the members of the staff, but only incidentally.

The major administrative problem considered by the Committee on Economic Security itself was that of the federal agencies which should be made responsible for the administration of the various parts of the social security program. This was a question which loomed large throughout the development of the program and one which seemed for a time likely to seriously divide the committee. Members of the technical board who were connected with the Federal Emergency Relief Administration believed that the committee should recommend the organization of a Cabinet Department of Public Welfare, to succeed the Federal Emergency Relief Administration and to bring together all activities of the federal government concerned with public assistance, public health, and similar aspects of public welfare.* Such a development was not favored, by the members of the technical board connected with the Department of Labor, who were very anxious that that department should retain jurisdiction over the United States Employment Service, the Children's Bureau, and the Women's Bureau, and also should be given responsibility for unemployment compensation.

The members of the Committee on Economic Security did not discuss this problem at any length in any of their formal

*This line of thinking ultimately was carried out in the establishment of the Department of Health, Education, and Welfare in 1953.—ED.

meetings. The matter was really settled in a personal conference between Secretary Perkins and Mr. Hopkins, with no one else present. At this conference, these two members of the committee reached an understanding that the time was not opportune to press for the organization of a Department of Public Welfare or to recommend any shifts of existing bureaus between departments. It was also agreed by them that unemployment compensation should come within the jurisdiction of the Department of Labor, and that the old age assistance grants should be under the jurisdiction of the Federal Emergency Relief Administration. This solution was thereafter accepted by all the members of the committee without further consideration. Some uncertainty prevailed until almost the time of the filing of the final report regarding the administration of the grants for aid to dependent children. For some time there were changes almost daily between the Children's Bureau and the Federal Emergency Relief Administration, but finally the responsibility for administering the aid to dependent children was allotted to the Federal Emergency Relief Administration. The other child welfare grants fell to the Children's Bureau and the grants for public health work to the United States Public Health Service.

As already recited, Congress upset these arrangements by making the Social Security Board an independent agency and by assigning to that board the functions which in the original bill were assigned to the Federal Emergency Relief Administration. This latter shift was accepted by the committee without serious objection, but it made every effort to keep the Social Security Board attached to the Department of Labor. This was also the wish of the President, as he advised members of the congressional committees who came to see him about the matter, but in the end he yielded to their desire that the Social Security Board be set up as an independent agency. The attention of the congressional

194

committee was called to the fact that this would leave the relations of the board to the United States Employment Service quite uncertain, but they did not deem it necessary to attempt to define these relations by law and considered it quite satisfactory that the United States Employment Service should be in the Department of Labor, while the Social Security Board was independent thereof.

The administration of unemployment compensation in the plan adopted by the Committee on Economic Security and Congress was primarily a state responsibility. Hence, the social security bill, at no stage, ever had much to say about the administration of unemployment compensation. The only provisions ever included in the bill were two conditions in Section 903 for the recognition of state laws for tax-offset purposes. These were: (1) that all compensation payments must be made through public employment offices; and (2) that the state system of administration must be satisfactory to the Social Security Board. As recited in the section on unemployment compensation, the condition relating to payments through public employment offices was modified by Congress to authorize payments also through other agencies approved by the Social Security Board. The other provision was considered by the people connected with the Committee on Economic Security to be one under which a great deal of authority would be given to the Social Security Board over the administration of unemployment compensation, but it was deemed unwise to say anything about this to the congressional committees. The temper of these committees was such that all federal control was under suspicion; but because nothing was said about the matter, this particular clause remained in the bill about as originally written.

Since the so-called old age insurance system was to be directly operated by the federal government, it was understood by everyone that this part of the bill would give rise to very serious administrative problems. Some consideration was given to the actual methods of collecting the taxes for old age insurance purposes. It was understood that two distinctly different methods existed in European countries, the stamp book and the payroll methods of collection. It was thought inadvisable, however, to prescribe in the congressional act which of these methods should be used. Instead, it was decided to write the law in such a way that either or both methods might be employed, as subsequent study might reveal to be desirable. The proposed bill provided that the taxes under Title VIII should not begin to accrue until January 1, 1937. The primary reason for this delay was to afford time for a more detailed study of the methods of administration and for the development of the necessary organization. It was always assumed by the "insiders" that the Social Security Board, after its organization, would send representatives to Europe to study in detail the European methods of administering old age insurance. Consequently, it was sought to keep the provisions in the bill relating to administration as flexible as possible. This was explained to the congressional committees and was entirely satisfactory to them.

A special administrative problem peculiar to our governmental organization related to the fact that the taxes in Title VIII and Title IX were made collectible by the Treasury Department, while the Social Security Board administered the old age benefits and passed upon the adequacy of the state unemployment compensation laws and their administration. Members of the staff who favored a national system of unemployment insurance sought to get away from this problem by proposing a governmental corporation, which was both to collect the taxes and administer the benefits. In regard to old age insurance, this was never proposed, as the staff members in charge of this study realized that the Treasury would never submit to collection of any federal taxes by any other agency. This was taken for granted by the

196

members of the Committee on Economic Security, as well as in Congress, and both the original and the final bill provided for the collection of the taxes by the Secretary of the Treasury. It was realized that, for the administration of the old age benefits under Title II, it would be necessary to have the records developed through the collection of the taxes under Title VIII. It was not considered necessary, however, to make any formal provisions for coöperation between these departments, as it was thought that this could be handled through interdepartmental agreements. Officials of the Treasury Department worked with the Committee on Economic Security in the drafting and redrafting of both these titles, and so it seemed to be a comparatively simple matter, not requiring any special legislation, to secure continued coöperation in the actual administration of the old age insurance system.

Appendices

APPENDIX I

*Executive Order Establishing the Committee on
Economic Security and the Advisory Council
on Economic Security*

By virtue of and pursuant to the authority vested in me by
the National Industrial Recovery Act (ch. 90, 48 Stat. 195),
I hereby establish (1) the Committee on Economic Security
(hereinafter referred to as the Committee) consisting of the
Secretary of Labor, chairman, the Secretary of the Treasury,
the Attorney General, the Secretary of Agriculture, and the
Federal Emergency Relief Administrator, and (2) the Advisory Council on Economic Security (hereinafter referred
to as the Advisory Council), the original members of which
shall be appointed by the President and additional members
of which may be appointed from time to time by the Committee.

The Committee shall study problems relating to the economic security of individuals and shall report to the President not later than December 1, 1934, its recommendations
concerning proposals which in its judgment will promote
greater economic security.

The Advisory Council shall assist the Committee in the
consideration of all matters coming within the scope of its
investigations.

The Committee shall appoint (1) a Technical Board on
Economic Security consisting of qualified representatives selected from various departments and agencies of the Federal Government, and (2) an executive director who shall
have immediate charge of studies and investigations to be
carried out under the general direction of the Technical
Board, and who shall, with the approval of the Technical

Board, appoint such additional staff as may be necessary to carry out the provisions of this order.

FRANKLIN D. ROOSEVELT

The White House
June 29, 1934.

(No. 6757)

APPENDIX II

Excerpt from "Minority Views"
on the Social Security Bill, 1935

The following statement was contained in House Committee Report No. 615, 74th Congress, 1st Session, April 5, 1935, to accompany H.R. 7260, pp. 43–44.

COMPULSORY OLD-AGE ANNUITIES

Title II provides for compulsory old-age annuities, and title VIII provides the method by which the money is to be raised to meet the expense thereof.

These two titles are interdependent, and neither is of any consequence without the other. Neither of them has relation to any other substantive title of the bill. Neither is constitutional. Therein lies one of the reasons for our opposition to them.

The Federal Government has no power to impose this system upon private industry.

The best legal talent that the Attorney General's office and the Brain Trust could marshal has for weeks applied itself to the task of trying to bring these titles within constitutional limitations. Their best effort is only a plain circumvention. They have separated the proposition into two titles. This separation is a separation in words only. There is no separation in spirit or intent. These two titles must stand or fall together.

The learned brief submitted by the Attorney General's Office contains in its summation the following weak, apologetic language:

There may also be taken into consideration the strong presumption which exists in favor of the constitutionality of an act of the Congress, in the light of which and of the foregoing discussion it is reasonably safe to assume that the social security bill, if enacted into law, will probably be upheld as constitutional.

We also oppose these two titles because they would not in any way contribute to the relief of present economic conditions, and might in fact retard economic recovery.

The original bill contained a title providing for voluntary annuities. This was another attempt to place the Government in competition with private business. Under fire, this title has been omitted. It was closely akin to title II. In fact, it had one virtue that title II does not possess in that it was voluntary while title II is compulsory.

These titles impose a crushing burden upon industry and upon labor.

They establish a bureaucracy in the field of insurance in competition with private business.

They destroy old-age retirement systems set up by private industries, which in most instances provide more liberal benefits than are contemplated under title II.

Appended hereto is a table showing the total taxes imposed under titles VIII and IX.

CONCLUSION

The minority membership of the Ways and Means Committee have at no time offered any political or partisan opposition to the progress of this measure, but on the contrary have labored faithfully in an effort to produce a measure that would be constitutional and that would insure to the general welfare of all the people.

Allen T. Treadway.
Isaac Bacharach.
Frank Crowther.
Harold Knutson.
Daniel A. Reed.
Roy O. Woodruff.
Thomas A. Jenkins.

APPENDIX III

*Letter of Transmittal and Summary of Major
Recommendations on Health Insurance from the
Committee on Economic Security to the President*

LETTER OF TRANSMITTAL

Washington, D.C.
November 6, 1935.

The President,
The White House.

Dear Mr. President:

In your address to the Conference on Economic Security on November 14, 1934, you said:

"There is also the problem of economic loss due to sickness—a very serious matter for many families with and without incomes, and therefore, an unfair burden upon the medical profession. Whether we come to this form of insurance soon or later on I am confident that we can devise a system which will enhance and not hinder the remarkable progress which has been and is being made in the practice of the professions of medicine and surgery in the United States."

The Committee on Economic Security has made careful studies of the problem of economic loss due to sickness, of American conditions and needs, and of measures which have been used to deal with the problem in America and in other countries. In its report of January 15th, 1935, the Committee made certain recommendations for the expansion of public health services to prevent ill health. These measures you recommended in your message of January 17th, 1935, to the Congress and they are now incorporated in the Social Security Act. Our recommendations on other measures for protection against sickness and against the costs of medical care were postponed at the request of advisers in the fields of medicine, hospital management and dentistry, in order to allow for more time to study the professional aspects of tentative proposals developed by the Committee's staff.

The Committee is now ready to make a further report on the provisions for certain types of public medical services and for Federal-State plans of insurance against loss of wages due to sickness and against the costs of medical care among the lower income groups of the population.

For several months the Committee has had the valuable counsel and assistance of experts in the fields of medicine, public health, hospital management, dentistry and nursing, and, on the subject of health insurance, of the staff of the Bureau of Medical Economics of the American Medical Association. The technical assistance rendered by members of these groups or their membership on the advisory boards and committees should not be interpreted as expressing their views either for or against legislation for health insurance. The report of our staff has also been reviewed by the appropriate committee of our Technical Board and by the Advisory Council appointed by you. The responsibility for the present report, however, rests solely with the Committee whose members have given careful consideration to the technical advice rendered as well as to various statements which have been made in response to invitations for expressions of opinion.

The present report contains a brief analysis of the need for meeting the economic losses due to sickness and a series of recommendations which deal with: (1) extension of public medical facilities and services, (2) insurance against loss of wages because of sickness and (3) insurance against the costs of medical care. Taken together, the recommendations presented in our report of January 15th and in the present report constitute, we believe, at least the beginnings of a national program for the protection of the population against disease, for the extension and improvement of medical care, and for the protection of the people against economic insecurity arising out of illness.

Our proposals on health insurance are especially cautious; they call for no drastic or hurried Federal action. In this field of social insurance, we are, in effect merely proposing that the Federal government shall undertake to give small financial aid to those states which develop systems of health insurance designed with due regard to necessary safeguards.

The Committee is hopeful that its report will serve as a basis for full discussion to the end that such differences of opinion as now exist may be resolved and eventuate in constructive legislation. However, the Committee does not believe that such legislation should be undertaken until there has been opportunity for extended discussion and further research by the Social Security Board.

> [signed]   Frances Perkins
>   Secretary of Labor (Chairman)
>   Henry Morgenthau, Jr.
>   Secretary of the Treasury
>   Homer S. Cummings
>   Attorney General
>   Henry A. Wallace
>   Secretary of Agriculture
>   Harry L. Hopkins
>   Federal Emergency Relief Administrator

SUMMARY OF MAJOR RECOMMENDATIONS

In our first report to the President we dealt with general and specific measures for economic security. In respect to risks which arise out of illness, we proposed certain particular measures—for child-care services, for child and maternal health services, and for a Nation-wide preventive public-health program to lessen the occurrence of sickness. We made only a progress report on other measures to protect wage-earners and their families against the costs of illness. These subjects were still being studied by our staff and our professional advisory committees.

In the present report we present our proposals on general measures to furnish economic security against sickness, dealing specifically with the development of public medical services and facilities, with insurance against wages lost through temporary disability, and with health insurance for wage-earners and their dependents. These proposals are:

1. With respect to Federal aid to State and local public medical facilities and services, we make the general recommendation that appropriate administrative action be taken and sufficient funds be made available, when necessary, to provide this aid. The surveys necessary to determine when and where Federal aid should be given are already under way in order that, if aid be deemed advisable, the required information will be at hand.

2. With respect to insurance against wage loss due to temporary disability (in the form of cash benefits), we recommend that this form of insurance should be provided in the same general manner as unemployment compensation. The members of our advisory committees and of our staff are unanimously in favor of the separate administration of insurance against wage loss and of insurance against the costs of medical care, and we are in agreement with this view.

3. We recommend that provision should be made for the further study of the occurrence of permanent disability and of measures to furnish protection against this risk.

4. With respect to insurance against the costs of medical care (medical benefits and so-called health insurance), we recommend a Federal-State permissive system in which any

208

State will receive a specified Federal subsidy, provided it meets certain basic Federal safeguards.

In submitting these recommendations we wish to make some general observations that appear to us to be pertinent.

Our plan for disability insurance would give assurance of some income to wage-earners who become disabled and would reduce the burdens which communities bear in the care of the disabled sick and the dependent.

Our design for health insurance leaves to the States the initiative in creating systems of insurance. The Federal Government would undertake to lay down general safeguards and to give financial aid to the States. The costs to the Federal Government would be small, especially in the light of the large benefits which would accrue to the national welfare.

On the subject of health insurance, our recommendations are especially conservative; but we believe that they offer a proper basis for the sound beginning of practices which will give to millions of men and women security against serious economic effects of sickness. Combined with the advantages of disability insurance, health insurance would free millions of families from the spectre of sickness costs.

Our plan for health insurance would give to those who need care easier access than they now have to those who are prepared to furnish the services. At the same time this plan would vastly reduce the burdens of medical costs to individual families and would increase and stabilize the incomes of practitioners and hospitals serving people of small and moderate means.

The system of health insurance which we recommend rests upon the basic principle that the private practice of medicine and of the allied professions should be conserved and strengthened. We have been especially careful to encourage high standards of professional service and to provide new incentives for their continued improvement. No single existing pattern, American or European, has been followed. Our proposals take account of experience at home and abroad and are designed to meet the needs of the American people under the conditions which exist in our States and local communities. In making this recommendation, we have carefully considered the interests not only of the public but also of the medical professions. We believe that these interests have been properly safeguarded and that our proposals are in accord with the views expressed by President Roosevelt in his address to the Conference on Economic Security, November 14, 1934, and will lead to "a system which will advance and not hinder the remarkable progress which has been made and is being made in the practice of the professions of medicine and surgery in the United States." We contemplate only those actions which will be quite as much in the interests of the members of the professions concerned with health and sickness as of the families with low incomes.

There still are broad gaps in our proposals; the measures we recommend will not give complete security against all the risks of illness nor will they meet the needs of all the people who need protection. There remains the need for more extended study of deficiencies in many communities in the supply of hospitals, of institutions for the chronic sick and of other necessary facilities, for a careful investigation of insurance to provide against *permanent* disability, and for study and experimentation on ways and means of giving protection to particular groups of people who cannot easily be served by the measures which have been proposed. We are confident, however, that we have devised proposals which will enhance the economic security of a large proportion of the population through the conservation of health and the mitigation of the economic burden laid upon families with low incomes by sickness and ill health. We therefore recommend that appropriate legislation be enacted.

APPENDIX IV

Selected Publications of Edwin E. Witte
on Social Security Problems, 1935–1937

SOCIAL SECURITY ACT—GENERAL

United States, House of Representatives, Committee on Ways and Means. *Economic Security Act.* Hearings on H.R. 4120, 74th Congress, 1st Session, January 21–February 12, 1935, pp. 2–9, 31–35, 56–79, 187–225, 237–253. (Opening Testimony, as Executive Director of the Committee on Economic Security.)

United States, Senate, Committee on Finance. *Economic Security Act.* Hearings on S. 1130, 74th Congress, 1st Session, January 22–February 20, 1935, pp. 31–35, 56–99, 187–225, 237–53.

"Features of the Economic Security Program," *Annals of the American Academy of Political and Social Science,* Vol. 178, pp. 88–94 (March, 1935).

"The Economic Security Act," in the *Book of States,* 1935 (published by the Council of American State Government and the American Legislator's Association), pp. 411–15.

"The National Social Security Program," *University of Wisconsin Alumni Magazine,* Vol. XXXVII, No. 4 (January, 1936), pp. 104–7.

"The Social Security Act," *Wisconsin Bar Association Proceedings,* Vol. 25, pp. 22–36 (1935).

Paying for Social Security (radio address, published and distributed by the National Municipal League, June, 1935).

"Economic Security and Life Insurance," *Manager's Magazine* (Hartford, Connecticut), Vol. X, No. 2, pp. 2–3 (March–April, 1935).

Book review of Abraham Epstein's *Insecurity, A Challenge to America,* Revised Edition, *Journal of Political Economy,* Vol. XLIX, No. 6, pp. 845–47 (December, 1936). (An answer to some of Epstein's criticisms of the Social Security Act.)

UNEMPLOYMENT COMPENSATION

"An Historical Account of Unemployment Insurance in the Social Security Act," *Law and Contemporary Problems,* Vol. III, No. 1, pp. 157–69 (January, 1936).

"The Essentials of Unemployment Compensation," *National Municipal Review,* Vol. XXV, No. 3, pp. 157–63 (March, 1936).

"Major Issues in Unemployment Compensation," *Social Service Review,* Vol. IX, No. 1, pp. 1–23 (March, 1935).

"Job Insurance—Its Limitations and Value," *Economic Forum,* Vol. II, No. 4, pp. 411–24 (Winter, 1935).

"The Unemployed in the Social Security Program," *Wharton Review,* Vol. VIII, No. 6, pp. 3–4, 16–17 (March, 1935).

"The Government and Unemployment," *American Labor Legislation Review,* Vol. XXV, No. 1 (March, 1935).

"Unemployment Compensation in Wisconsin," *Labor Information Bulletin* (U.S. Bureau of Labor Statistics), Vol. III, No. 8, pp. 4–5 (August, 1936).

OLD AGE SECURITY

"Old Age Security in the Social Security Act," *Journal of Political Economy,* Vol. XLV, No. 1 (February, 1937), pp. 1–44.

"In Defense of the Federal Old Age Benefit Plan," *Social Security Analyst,* Vol. I, No. 1, pp. 7–8, 24–25 (January, 1937). Also in *American Labor Legislation Review,* Vol. XXVII, No. 1 (January, 1937).

"Are Old Age Pensions Worth Their Cost?" *American Labor Legislation Review,* Vol. XXVI, No. 1 (March, 1936), pp. 7–14.

"Old Age Security," *National Municipal Review,* Vol. XXIV, No. 7, pp. 371–74 (July, 1935).

"Financing Social Security: Reserves versus Current Taxation" (address at the annual meeting of the Tax Policy League [December, 1936] included in the proceedings of this meeting published by this organization under the title *How Shall Business Be Taxed?*).

"Planned Security for an Older Population," *New York Times,* February 17 and 21, 1935.

"Pensions and the Social Security Act," *News from the Wisconsin Conference of Social Work,* Vol. III, No. 1, pp. 2–4 (January 25, 1936). (On Wisconsin legislation.)

"Why the Townsend Old Age Pension Plan is Impossible," U.S. House of Representatives, Ways and Means Committee; Hearings on the *Economic Security Act,* Jan.–Feb., 1935 (74th Congress, 1st Session), pp. 894–96; also in *Congressional Record,* April 12, 1935, Vol. 79, pp. 5548–49).

"What's Wrong with the Townsend Plan," N.E.A. Feature Article, published in the (Madison, Wis.) *Capital Times,* January 23, 24, 26, 1936, and in many other newspapers.

MISCELLANEOUS

"Social Insurance in Europe during the Depression," *American Labor Legislation Review,* Vol. XXV, No. 4, pp. 158–64, (December, 1935).

The Relation of Relief to Society (radio address, November, 1935, distributed by the Wisconsin Emergency Relief Administration, 7 pages, mimeographed).

Index

Forster, H. Walter, 105n, 106n, 157, 158, 160, 161
Frank, Jerome, 71, 72, 77, 127, 136n, 137n
Frankfurter, Felix, 16, 42n, 63
Fuller, Claude A., 93, 132

Garner, John N., 106n
Gaus, John, 14n
George, Walter F., 105, 106, 107, 161
Gerry, Peter G., 104, 170
Gill, Corrington T., 13, 14, 16, 22, 24, 25, 65
Givens, Meredith B., 14n, 15, 31
Glover, James W., 34
Goldmark, Josephine, 118n, 119n
Gore, Thomas P., 106
Government workers, 131
Graham, Frank P., 44, 49, 56, 58n, 62, 85, 87n, 120n
Green, William, 3, 49, 51, 54, 56, 58n, 59n, 61, 62, 82, 87, 88, 130, 136n
Greenough, Robert B., 180, 181n
Greenway, Isabella, 99n
Guffey, Joseph F., 104
Gulick, Luther, 14n

Haas, George C., 73, 150
Hale, Frederick, 105
Hall, Helen, 3, 52, 53, 58n, 62, 85
Halsey, Olga S., 23n, 189
Hamilton, Mr. (Equitable Life), 106n, 157, 158
Hamilton, Walton H., 16, 23, 25, 36
Hansen, Alvin H., 4n, 16, 23, 24, 25, 26, 27, 82, 118, 137n
Harriman, Henry I., 88, 89n
Harris, Joseph P., 33, 56, 92n, 98, 116, 126
Harris, S. R., 28n, 193
Harrison, George M., 49, 51, 54, 58n, 62
Harrison, Pat, 79, 89n, 95n, 102n, 103, 104, 105, 106n, 107, 164
Hastings, Daniel O., 105, 151, 152
Health insurance, 21, 27, 30, 40, 82n, 167, 172, 173–89, 205, 206, 207, 208, 209, 210

Heer, Clarence, 33
Hill, Lister, 71n, 93, 107, 134, 139, 142
Hoar, Roger S., 134n
Holtzoff, Alexander, 22, 24, 25, 27, 33n, 65, 70
Homeopaths, 176, 177
Hopkins, Harry L., 8, 9, 11, 15, 19n, 44, 59, 64, 65, 68, 70, 73, 78n, 82, 118, 149, 207; health insurance, 174, 187; old age insurance, 152; pooled funds, 127; public welfare department, 139, 194; social security and work program, 77
Horlick, Mr. (Equitable Life), 106n, 157, 158
Hospital Advisory Committee, 176
Howe, Louis, 19n
Hudson, Glenn, 85
Huggins, George A., 154
Hunter, Joel D., 52, 53, 58n

Illinois Manufacturers' Association, 90
Industrial Relations Counselors, Inc., 29
Invalidity insurance, 21, 28n, 189
Irwin, Robert B., 191

Jackson, Henry E., 103n
Jenkins, Thomas A., 204
Jensen, Edward W., 23, 24, 26
Julian, William A., 4n

Kaufman, Mr. (National Retail Dry Goods Assn.), 89n
Keller, Helen, 192
Keller, Kent E., 79
Kellogg, Paul, 5n, 49, 52, 55, 56, 57, 58n, 61, 62, 85, 123, 130
Kennedy, Thomas, 118n, 119n
Keyes, Henry W., 107
Keyserling, Leon H., 77
King, William H., 103n, 105, 106, 107, 161
Kjaer, S. J., 28n
Knutson, Harold, 204
Kulp, Clarence, 85
Kurtz, Mr. (Vocational Rehabilitation), 189

216

217

tirement annuities, 21, 146; state vs. federal, 143, 144, 145
Old age security, 26, 27, 29, 30, 44, 46, 47, 61, 67, 82n, 85, 99, 212
Old Age Security Committee, 24, 29
Oliphant, Herman J., 16, 23, 25
Organized labor, 16n, 48, 49, 87, 106, 138, 139n, 161
Osteopaths, 176

Palmer, Gladys, 31
Parker, L. H., 92n, 100
Parran, Thomas, Jr., 175n, 181n
Pence, Mr. (YMCA), 155
Pensions, 46, 204; blind, 164; church, 154, 155; industrial, 102, 106, 157, 158, 159, 160, 161; old age, 51, 101, 130
Perkins, Frances, 5n, 7, 13, 15, 16, 17, 19n, 37, 42, 43, 44, 46, 47, 48, 49, 59, 64, 65, 68, 74, 76n, 79, 81, 82, 88n, 96, 100, 101, 102, 118, 138, 139n, 140, 149, 150, 168, 181, 188, 201, 207; advisory council, 50, 51, 54, 55, 121; committee staff and tasks, 20, 28, 111, 127; conference tasks, 120n; dependent children, 164; final report, 70, 71, 72; health insurance, 174, 178, 187; old age insurance, 152, 153; public welfare, 194; unemployment compensation, 126; Wagner-Lewis bill, 3
Persons, Frank, 14n, 139n
Policy-making of committee, 18, 19, 20, 66, 67, 70, 73, 121
Powell, O. S., 32, 137n
Public assistance, 61, 139, 162, 193
Public employment, 27, 31
Public Employment and Relief Committee, 24
Public health, 67, 77, 84n, 171–73, 181, 183, 193, 205, 208
Public Health Advisory Committee, 176
Public relations, 7, 35, 41, 42, 46, 51, 59, 189
Public welfare, federal, 71n, 139, 193, 194
Public works, 113n, 128

Railroad Retirement Act, 13, 100, 142
Raskob, John J., 4n, 16, 19n
Raushenbush, Paul, 135n, 141n
Reagh, Mr. (Treasury), 150, 152
Reed, Daniel A., 204
Reitz, Henry L., 34
Relief problem, 11, 12, 21, 27, 31, 61, 71n, 145
Religious organizations, 52, 53, 97n, 154, 155, 165, 166, 167, 168, 169, 170
Research studies, 14n, 23, 207
Reybourn, Samuel W., 89
Rice, Stuart, 23, 24
Richberg, Donald, 16
Richter, Otto C., 34, 35, 150
Riefler, Winfield W., 23, 24, 25, 27, 117, 118, 137n
Robinson, Joseph T., 106n
Roche, Josephine, 23, 25, 27, 50, 51, 53, 64, 65, 82, 127, 128, 187, 188
Roosevelt, Franklin D., 3, 4, 8, 9, 11, 16n, 19, 42, 45, 67, 68, 69, 73, 74, 76, 77, 78, 90n, 94, 108, 121, 129, 137, 139, 142, 150, 168, 171, 176n, 177, 186, 194, 201, 202, 205, 207, 210; advisory council members, 48–53; amendments, 101, 140, 162; committee members, 8; comprehensive social security, 5, 6, 7, 17, 18, 79, 97; contributions, 7, 18, 111, 119, 128; health insurance, 174, 188; maternal and child health, 166; old age insurance, 7, 18, 46, 47, 95, 149, 160; reconstruction and recovery, 6; reserve funds, 7, 18, 111, 119; stabilization of employment, 75, 111, 119, 128; state-federal system, 7, 54, 111, 118, 119, 120, 128; Townsend plan, 99n
Roper, Daniel L., 44
Ross, Emerson, 31, 71n, 115n
Rowe, Davies, 14n
Rubinow, I. M., 3, 82n
Russell amendment, 106, 143
Ryan, John A., 53, 58n

Scharrenberg, Paul, 49, 51, 54, 56, 58n
Scientific institutions, 154, 155, 156
Sheppard-Towner Act, 165, 166, 167
Sherwin, Belle, 49, 51, 58n
Shipman, George A., 33, 116, 193
Shoup, Carl, 33
Simons, A. M., 179, 180, 185
Social credit, 28n
Social Science Research Council, 14n
Social Security Act, 47n, 84n, 88n, 97, 99, 104, 105, 106, 108
Social security, comprehensive, 5, 66n, 72, 73, 74, 89n, 96, 97n
Stabilization of employment, 75, 111, 119, 128, 130, 134, 141
Stam, C. F., 92n, 100
Stark, Louis, 59, 60n, 76n
Stewart, Bryce W., 12n, 14n, 15, 29, 55, 56, 59n, 60, 112, 116, 118, 121, 122, 123, 125, 138, 193
Story, Harold W., 82, 89n, 118n, 119n
Studebaker, John W., 190
Survivors' insurance, 21, 28n
Sweezy, Alan R., 33, 64n
Swope, Gerard J., 16, 19n, 49, 50, 90n
Sydenstricker, Edgar L., 12n, 30, 31, 166, 172, 174, 175, 176, 178, 179, 180, 181, 182, 185, 186, 187, 188

Taber, Louis J., 50, 51, 54, 58n
Taylor, Mr., 14n
Teagle, Walter C., 16, 49, 50, 60n, 90n
Technical board, 8, 9, 20, 21, 22–27, 31, 37, 38, 39, 64, 65, 66, 67, 70, 112, 114, 115, 116, 117, 118, 121, 122, 125, 137n, 162, 172, 189, 192, 193, 201
Thrift Foundation, 152
Tolley, H. R., 16, 23, 24, 25, 26
Townsend plan, 28n, 35, 85, 86, 95, 96, 98, 99, 103n, 140
Training for jobs, 21
Treadway, Allen T., 107, 134n
Tugwell, Rexford G., 4n, 16, 19n, 65, 71, 72, 127, 187

Turner, Mr. (Sen. Clark's law partner), 161
Tydings, Millard, 106
Tyson, Mr., 85

Unemployment insurance, 21, 27, 29, 30, 32, 44, 45, 46, 47, 55, 56, 57, 58n, 59, 60n, 66, 67, 68, 73, 83n, 84n, 90n, 94, 95, 103n, 174, 194, 208, 212; businessmen, 89n, 127, 132, 133; contributions, 7, 57, 58, 59, 61, 62, 73, 85, 111, 112, 113, 119, 122, 123, 124, 125, 127, 130, 132, 193; exemptions, 131, 132, 141, 143, 156; pooled funds, 28, 101, 112, 113, 114, 119n, 122, 125n, 127, 135, 141, 142; relation to relief, 89n, 113, 115; reserve funds, 4n, 7, 18, 22, 27, 28n, 32, 116, 119, 126, 134, 136n, 137n, 138n, 193; state-federal systems, 7, 18, 54, 56, 60n, 71, 111, 112, 114, 115, 116, 117, 118, 119, 119n, 120, 121, 122, 124, 125n, 138, 140, 141, 193, 195; state laws, 72n, 115, 123, 125, 128, 129, 133, 134, 135, 142; subsidy plan, 56, 57, 58, 59, 60n, 62, 84n, 85, 86, 87, 88n, 115, 116, 117, 118, 119n, 120n, 121, 122, 124, 126, 130, 131; tax-offset plan, 83n, 115, 129, 130, 131, 133, 135, 140, 195; voluntary plans, 50, 112
Unemployment Insurance Committee, 24, 39, 57, 59, 112, 117, 118, 122
Unemployment Reserve Funds Committee, 25, 32
United States
Agricultural Adjustment Administration (AAA), 21, 32
Bureau of the Budget, 102
Business Advisory and Planning Council (Dept. of Commerce), 4n, 50, 60n, 89n, 90n, 125, 137n
Children's Bureau, 163, 165, 166, 167, 168, 171, 183, 193, 194
Department of Agriculture, 32
Department of Health, Education and Welfare, 193n

219

Department of Labor, 12, 15, 17n, 101, 102, 122, 123, 133, 138, 139, 140, 142, 143, 163, 193, 194
Department of the Treasury, 66, 72, 77, 102, 133, 137n, 196, 197
Employment Service, 139n, 193, 195
Federal Coördinator of Transportation, 13
Federal Emergency Relief Administration (FERA), 9, 12, 17n, 31, 145, 162, 163, 193, 194
Federal Reserve Board, 137n, 138n
House of Representatives Rules Committee, 98
House of Representatives Ways and Means Committee, 144, 163, 204
National Planning Committee, 10n
National Recovery Administration (NRA), 21
National Resources Board (and Committee), 6, 10, 21
Post Office Department, 102
Public Health Service, 84, 165, 166, 167, 172, 173
Senate Finance Committee, 159
Senate Labor Committee, 80
Social Security Board, 10, 101, 102, 139, 142, 143, 145, 163, 182, 185, 189, 194, 195, 196, 207
Supreme Court, 100
Women's Bureau, 193

Valgren, Victor N., 23, 24
Van Kleeck, Mary, 85, 86
Van Nuys, Frederick, 79

Veteran's Pension Act, 163
Viner, Jacob, 16, 23, 24, 25, 27, 65, 117, 118, 137n
Vinson, Fred M., 81n, 91, 93, 95n, 134, 139, 158, 163, 164

Wagner, Monsignor (National Catholic Welfare Conference), 168
Wagner, Robert F., 16, 77, 79, 81, 88n, 105, 131, 191
Wagner labor disputes bill, 4, 88n
Wagner-Lewis bill, 3, 4, 5, 7, 45, 56, 58n, 59, 79, 84n, 88n, 112n, 115, 116, 117, 118, 119n, 120n, 122, 124, 126, 132, 136n
Wallace, Henry A., 64, 65, 71, 72, 127, 137n, 187, 207
Walsh, David I., 104, 107n
Weigert, Oscar, 14n
West, Congressman (former), 106n
Wilcox, Mr. (Treasury), 77, 92n, 100, 150, 161
Willetts, Joseph H., 118n
Williams, Aubrey, 16, 23, 24, 26, 65, 70, 71n, 162
Williamson, W. R., 34, 35, 55, 122
Wilson, Rev. (Christian Church), 155
Wilson, M. L., 16
Winant, John G., 50, 51, 54, 56
Winship, Blanton, 102
Women's organizations, 51, 85, 97n, 165, 167
Woodruff, Roy O., 93, 190, 204
Workmen's compensation, 28n
Work relief bill, 77, 78n, 88n, 94, 139
World Court, 94
Wrigley, William P., Jr., 50

Young, Owen D., 19n, 50